Northern Outpost

M. S. Thomas

Tellwell Talent
www.tellwell.ca

ISBN
978-0-2288-8814-7 (Hardcover)
978-0-2288-8813-0 (Paperback)
978-0-2288-8815-4 (eBook)

Table of Contents

ONE

The wedding was over. In the basement of the church, the one hundred guests had been served supper by the church ladies. The speeches had been made and the guests were just finishing their coffee. I slipped into a side room to change into my going away outfit.

The suit that I was putting on was light tan with dark brown trims. I should have known by these colors that the suit was a bad omen and the marriage was eventually going to fail. I later found out that with my dark hair and light skin that I was a "winter" color and that I should only wear purple, blue, green, red, hot pink and steel grey. The tan suit with the dark brown trim was not my thing.

When I was in high school, my mother had bought me a dark brown plaid suit that she had seen in Woodward's window. I never liked wearing that suit. It was the brown color. The next year she bought me a grey suit with a white pin stripe that she had also seen in Woodward's window as she passed that window each day in her lunch hour when she went from her job to the shopping. I wore that grey suit until it was almost hanging by a thread.

My new husband, Bob and I had the use of a car that was kept by his parents, Daniel and Lois, in a private garage in the city. The car was for use to use when they came to the city and also for taking any car vacations. So we said goodbye to the guests and Bob drove us from the church to a motel on the north side of the city. The time was getting late and I was tired after the strain of the wedding. When we got inside the motel room, Bob sat in a chair and started to discuss our wedding. I went into the bathroom and changed into the thin fancy lace see-through night dress that I had purchased for the wedding night. When I came out I was expecting Bob to be overwhelmed and ravish me to him like always happens in a love novel. He didn't seem to be impressed with my flimsy nightgown and really didn't pay attention. I was crushed. So I had to sit and converse with him. We finally went to bed. The next morning we stopped in to say goodbye to my mother and started on the honeymoon to Arizona.

Bob and I had met at a fall dance at the university. I had finished my degree in nursing but Bob had one more year to go. I had to work one year in the province and in my field to satisfy the government for the money that they had given me each month in my last year, but the money did not have to be paid back as it was not a loan. At the dance we got along well and Bob asked me if he could take me out following this event. So each night after we did some studying, Bob would come to my house and take me out walking. My mother and I lived close to the university, so it was quite convenient for Bob.

We usually walked on White Avenue and looked in the shop windows. Across the street was a dance hall but we never went there. Later on, one of the bank managers who came to the northern hamlet had gone there and had danced with a young lady but did not get a contact number for her so that he could take her out. A few days later he decided that he definitely wanted to see her again. So he went to that dance hall every Friday and Saturday night to see if she would come back there. The wait lasted almost a year, but finally she came to the dance and he was able to reconnect with her and later married her. They were very happy together.

Bob was having trouble with his English essays as he had gone to school in the north whereas I had gone to a city school and was quite good at English including grammar. We were drilled in grammar and each day the blackboards would be filled with fill in the blank grammar lessons. When I was in high school I had tutored a young girl in English. She went on to become a newspaper reporter and wrote articles every day for the public to read.

In grade school we had in our class each year a student called George. George sat at the back corner of the class, didn't get asked any questions by the teacher, and never passed a grade with us. However, George was always "recommended" for the next year, so he was in our class with us the next year and every year. George couldn't play baseball when we played because he was big, awkward, and would fall down. George was an only child. His parents owned a main line food company and one day George would own it, so he had to be educated. George always had a tutor. In high school, I lost track of George because we had moved to another school district, but when I got to university, I could not believe my eyes, because there was George dressed in a black university style gown. No doubt George still had a tutor, maybe more than one, but he was going to make it.

So knowing that tutoring worked well, I started tutoring Bob in English. He managed to pass on the basis that his English writing had improved so much over the year that he was doing well. The special attention had worked and he managed to graduate.

I loved the city even though we went almost every week to my uncle's Bill's farm. My cousins on the farm got my sister and me helping to make ice cream. We got ice from the ice house where the ice was put in the winter time and where it lasted all year to keep the ice box in the house supplied and to make the ice cream. The ice cream, made with fresh pure cream was really spectacular. Of my three cousins, the oldest, Harry, played the saxophone by ear. His father had taken him to the city for lessons, but the teacher said that he could not teach the boy to read music as everything was in his head. Harry had played for the dances for years, but as time went on, younger players came into the band and they could all read music. Harry did not fit in by only playing by ear so he had to quit. He called the younger music readers "the young punks". Harry still played his saxophone at home and his sister who did all the cooking on the farm played the piano. The youngest cousin, in my opinion, beat them all because he had taught himself to yodel.

The farm had a horse called Kate. When we went to the farm to visit, Kate would stand at the fence and wait almost all day for one of us to climb the fence and get on her. She loved us and loved to give us rides. My youngest cousin, Ray, the yodeller, took me out on Kate one day and I rode behind him and hung on to his jacket. We went on the dirt road away out beyond the back quarter. Then it started to pour rain. The rain was so heavy that we couldn't see. The horse was slipping and sliding on the muddy wet road. I was six years old, frightened, and started to cry. Ray said "Don't cry! I will drop the reins and Kate will take us home". The horse did. A horse will always get home to the barn. I sometimes dreamed that Kate was coming for us in the northern outpost to take us back to the city.

TWO

When we got back from the honeymoon and to the city, Bob did the buying for the store. Then the night before we were to leave he put the loaner car back in the rented garage and we packed up the wedding presents. The train to the north only went once a week. That meant that the town only got fresh fruit and vegetables once a week. Bob had told me that we would go to the northern town for one year to let his parents take a trip to Britain. What a ruse that was. We would be staying in his parent's house until they returned and maybe after that for some time.

The morning that we were to leave the city, we said goodbye to my mother who wasn't working that day because it was Saturday. She had tears in her eyes. We took a taxi to the train station.

Years before, my sister and I had persuaded my mother to get a job with the railway because then we could get free rides on the train. In those days the employees got 3 or 4 free passes a year. She was, at the time, working as the manager of the credit department at a stylish dress shop on 101 Street in the city.

"But they have an exam" my mother said. "Well, get out the typewriter and practice" we said. So she practiced for a month, typing and reviewing her Pittman shorthand and passed the exam with flying colors. She now had a job with the railway. My sister and I were happy, looking forward to free rides.

So when we got to the train station, I showed Bob the window on the second floor where my mother worked for her boss. The window was at the front of the station and that window looked out on the street. Her friend, Joan, worked on the other side of the second floor and her window looked out over the platform and the rail lines. There wasn't any air conditioning so in the summer the workers had to open the windows. When the trains went by, all the smoke from the coal burning trains went up and in Joan's window. It wasn't long before Joan started getting pulmonary disease and a frequent cough that got worse as time went on. From Joan's window she saw one day a trainman move off the tracks for an oncoming train, but when he stepped onto the tracks next to him, he was hit and killed by another oncoming train. The trains were going slowly in the yard, but he still got killed. He left a wife and 4 small children. We knew this man because we all went to the same high school. When the school had a concert, this man, when a student, would give a drum solo and he was a fantastic drummer. The drums would now be silent.

Bob and I watched that our baggage and wedding gifts were loaded into the baggage car of the train going north. Then we boarded the train and got a seat at the back of the coach car. The trainman loaded onto the train a large cooler that contained pop and sandwiches to be sold to the passengers. He and the engineer had this little business going on the side. The passengers didn't mind as there was not a diner car on the train.

The train was very small with only an engine, one passenger car, one baggage car and a caboose. It was the N. A. R. short for Northern Alberta Railway. The trainman doubled as the conductor and he and the engineer were the only two workers on the train. The ride was going to take all day. The only other passengers on the train were a group at the front of the coach.

The engine started and went slowly through the yard of tracks. Then it went a little faster as we got away from the city. We stopped at every town as we went north so that mail and baggage could be unloaded. I knew when we got to the muskeg because the train started to get rough, to bounce and sway side to side. Bob recognized the passengers who were at the front of the coach. They lived in the town and shopped at the store that his parents owned. So I was left by myself and Bob went forward to cultivate these people to help make future business for the store. Then, at a fairly dry place in the muskeg, the train stopped and so did my heart. Here we were out in the wide open area with muskeg all around. However, I need not have had to worry because the trainman passed out some shallow containers and everyone got off the train to pick berries. The passengers picked Saskatoon berries and a few strawberries. We were not anywhere near Saskatoon, but that is what the berries were called. I was very surprised at the train stopping to let the passengers pick berries but this is what always happened. The passengers got back on the train and we continued on for a few hours. Then the train stopped again and the same thing took place. Back on the train, everyone dived in and ate their berries.

When we got going again, Bob was once more laughing and visiting with the people that he knew. I was left by myself.

I found out later that one of the older ladies that he was talking with had a German shepherd dog. This dog had a real bed to sleep on and when she ordered a side of beef, the dog got to eat the front quarter and she ate the better cuts from the back quarter. The other dogs in the town only got dog food.

We finally came to the end of the line which was three miles from the main town. Bob's mother met us and drove us to what was to be our home for a year, I thought. When I got into Bob's room which was now our room, it was like going back in time. There were high school textbooks on the window ledge and pennants on the walls. The family had bought for me a five foot long fibreglass fishing rod, similar to what they used. So when the weekend came we went fishing. I was surprised that Bob was going to work eighty hours a week and I would be home alone for that time. He did come home for lunch and supper but that was a gobble and run affair.

We fished for pickerel and pike and I got to taste pickerel cheeks that were a delicacy in many large cities. The north was loaded with mosquitoes that did not bother the family, as they had had a taste of them for a long time, but I was new blood and they came after me with gusto. I had to keep my jacket zipped up to my neck and a scarf over my head even though it was hot so the only skin showing was my face and hands. Lois had made the picnic lunch and she always made a good one.

When we got home, I was feeling sick and went to bed. Lois said that I had sun stroke. But when I vomited the next morning, I realized that I was pregnant. So, I did not have sun stroke, but had SON stroke. The pregnancy must have happened on the honeymoon or the night on our return, when we were sleeping at my mother's house, and the foot of the bed collapsed and hit the floor with a bang.

The family owned the lot on the corner and it was beside the house. They drove the car onto that lot and parked it near the side door. To get from the car to the door you had to climb up on a packing crate, step over the top of the fence and climb down on another packing crate. When I was four months pregnant, I missed the second packing crate and fell. I was not hurt, but the same afternoon, Daniel, Bob's father, had the local carpenter put in a gate. Why a gate had not been put there before, I had no idea.

The house was a bungalow style and had a front vestibule but that door was only used when company came. The side door was always used and it was half way down to the basement. The basement only had a dirt floor but it was well tamped down. There was a water barrel that was filled each week by the water truck. If you were lucky, in the summer time you also had water in a rain barrel outside. Also in the basement were two barrels filled with sand where the garden vegetables were put to keep them for the winter. Upstairs were the two bedrooms and a small bathroom. Only cold water came to this bathroom. The toilet was a chemical toilet and few times a week, lime was put in it to keep the odor down. When the toilet needed emptying, it was dumped onto the garden for fertilizer.

The kitchen did not have any eating space and it was so small that the refrigerator had to be in the dining room. The stove was an oil stove and I had to learn how to use it. That type of stove did have a good baking oven. The cold water from the basement also came to a tap in the kitchen and had to be heated on the stove.

The living room and dining room were connected with an arch. The floors were dark brown wood and there were linoleum squares that almost reached to the edges of the two rooms. There was not a fireplace in the living room. Besides having the refrigerator in the dining room, there was a tea wagon with a silver tea set on top and as far as I knew, this was never used.

The house had an upstairs but it had never been finished. I would rather have had this upstairs finished than to have an unused tea wagon and precious tea set in the dining room.

THREE

Lois, my mother- in- law was from London. Long before I had gotten to the town, she had started up a group that was for the purpose of raising money to give scholarships to students. The organization was similar to a group in the United Kingdom. Since I was fifth generation Canadian this wasn't really my thing, but i had to belong. Lois was the head of the group and it wasn't long before I was elected as secretary. The group met once a month at her house and did a few projects to make some money which was used to put out the scholarships for the school pupils, so it was a worthy cause. One of the ladies who came to the group talked about her family. She had nine children. She had almost died having the eighth baby, but the priest came to her house to see her and to encourage her to have another child. He was a big influence. She almost died again when she had the ninth baby. The children were all boys and one of the older boys, on a Monday, had to stay home from school to help with the washing. This mother said that she washed her kitchen floor every day. She was cleaner than any of the rest of us. Then we learned that there were mattresses leaning against her kitchen walls and in the evening they were put down on the floor as beds for all the children. That is why she had to wash the kitchen floor so often.

One of the things that the group did was to help at the fair grounds on July 1, which at that time was called Dominion Day. Some of the local people fed their young children blue berries prior to the event. These children then got diarrhoea and had to go to the hospital. The parents were then free to go to the gala which was outdoors at the fairgrounds. To raise money, our group purchased a pretty doll in a box and decorated over the skirt with quite a few fifty dollar bills. Fifty dollars was quite a bit of money at that time. This doll was an appealing raffle prize and we did not need a license in those days to have a raffle. My job was to carry the doll around and Lois was with me to sell the tickets. We made quite a bit of money with that one prize.

We also made and sold the hot dogs that we even buttered. We couldn't sell the watermelon because it was too hard for women to cut. After I had displayed the doll, I worked making hot dogs until I almost looked like a hot dog. Our group rented from the big city the equipment to make cotton candy. We were sent an aluminum tub about two and a half feet in diameter and some paper cones. The tub was electric and the power company arranged for us to have power. We made some sugar syrup and put some in the tub. To make the candy, the tub spun around and we ran a paper cone around the top and the cotton candy stuck to the cone. This cotton candy was popular and also a money maker. The celebration went on into the night with drinking and a dance. The people in one family in the town were all brittle diabetics. But they loved the first of July and they loved dancing. By the morning, these people were all passed out cold. If the doctor had not known of them, they would have been thought to be drunk and left to sober up. But the doctor knew that they needed some insulin shots to get them out of diabetic coma, otherwise they would die. One year in the future, some of them were going to die, but not this year.

There wasn't any recycling in those days so lots of good things were taken to the dump. The dump was free to take things there and if you wanted something, you just helped yourself. One woman with small children went to the dump every day at lunch time to eat and feed the children. The sisters at the Catholic rectory took the family food, but she still went to the dump to make sure that they weren't missing out on something edible and tasty.

So the next big celebration of the summer was that the town put on a formal tea at the dump. The men who worked at the dump checked the wind direction so the dump odor would not get to the tea. They also put up strings with flags on them so the birds would not fly over and drop little packages. There were not any rats about because the Alberta people worked very hard to keep the province rat free.

Three long tables were set up and smaller tables with chairs set around so the people could sit and sip their tea. All of the tables had white tablecloths on them. Lois, my mother- in- law, was invited to be one of three women to sit at the tables and serve the tea. Fancy tea cups and saucers were spread out over the tables. There were sandwiches, cookies, and cakes to eat. Everything was very fancy.

Everyone came dressed in their best. The weather was not too hot so the men came in suits and some of the ladies wore long dresses. The mayor came in a tuxedo.

The optometrist was in town on the day of the dump tea. I had been driving him about so that he could visit some of his clients that were in the south hamlet that was three miles away and I also drove him to the tea at the dump. We were chatting. By not paying much attention, I had driven the optometrist through a ditch. He was shocked and said,"I think you should come to see me to get some glasses." So when the mayor was on the platform and my eyes were not the greatest, I thought that in his black and white outfit he looked like a penguln. I then knew that the eye man was certainly right.

The mayor gave a very fitting speech. He said that the purpose of the tea was to show the people that the garbage depot was very important. He praised the dump workers for keeping such a tidy dump because the tidiness was then an example to the town to keep the whole area, including the town, clean and neat. There was great clapping for the mayor. He really cut a fine figure in his tuxedo.

There was only one bad incident of the afternoon. One of the ladies, not Lois, serving the tea knocked over her teapot. All the tea spilled out. Instead of her being concerned about the spoiled tablecloth, she was only concerned about her expensive dress. She jumped up and yelled" My dress, my dress." Otherwise the day was a great success. We were all proud of our dump.

When everyone was going home, the children were given some of the leftover food and a balloon.

The mayor shook hands with most of the people. He really did look outstanding in his tuxedo even though it was a little snug. I praised Lois for the job that she had done by helping to make the day such a success. I had to keep in the good books with her.

FOUR

The main street where the stores were had one or two lots between stores. That was so that if there was a fire, the entire town would not burn down. The store that we had, was first owned by Daniel and his partner. They also owned the smaller store three miles to the south. It was Daniel's job to go through the bush each night to bank the fire in that store. In the wintertime, he went on snowshoes.. The partner was older than Daniel and suddenly died. Daniel did not have the money to buy out the half of the store that was available from the partner.

But one night in the middle of the night the store three miles away caught fire. The manager of that store lived close by and before the fire got too far along, managed to get the books out of the store. One of the books had the names of all the people who owed money to the store so this money could be collected now. The store burned to the ground because by the time that the volunteer fire department got organized and went the three miles to the fire, the situation was hopeless as far as saving the building went but the store was insured.

In the outpost town, there was not a fire inspector nor was there an insurance inspector. Thus there wasn't anybody to investigate any arson with that fire. So the insurance money from that store fire was paid out to Daniel. What a godsend! Now he could buy out the other half of the store left by his partner so that he now owned the whole store. The smaller store three miles away was never rebuilt. That manager who had saved the books came to work at the main store.

The general store across from our store was owned by the Scotsman. He had sayings for a lot of his customers. When I went into his store, he would say," Here comes Mrs. Ducket with her bucket". I don't know where he got his sayings. He and his wife liked to put on dinner parties. Bob and I were always invited. On Burn's night we got to eat haggis with turnips and mashed potatoes. There was always lots of scotch shortbread and quite rich food. After dinner we often played bridge. One time we were playing and the bank manager and his wife were there. The wife was almost full term in her pregnancy. Suddenly her water broke with a splash onto the rug. What a mess. That was the end of the bridge for that night. The baby didn't come for a few days more, but that had been the signal that it was soon to be in this world. One afternoon, the Scotsman was waiting in a lineup at a theatre in the city when he had a heart attack and fell over dead. His son, who was about fourteen at the time, was with him in the lineup. He had to phone home to the northern hamlet to ask what to do. After he was buried, his wife continued to operate the store. They also owned quite a bit of property in the town, most of it commercial. I had saved some money in the year that I had worked before I got to the outpost and I wanted to buy one or two lots. Then, if the town boomed,

I would make a good profit. But the family would not let me buy anything because they said that they already owned a lot of property. That didn't help me but I had to abide by what they said.

I did a lot for that family. Daniel had ordered a new boat, a little bigger than the present one. It came from the east on the train. The boat had hoops for the top and I sewed a canvas top to go over the hoops to hold off any rain.

I also designed a cushion cover that would be attractive to tourists. The store sold thousands of them. Also, one season I got the store to order artificial flowers, some shallow vases, and some foam. With these materials I made bouquets of flowers that the store could sell. Because it was wintertime and the country was all snow, the store sold at least one to every home sometimes two Again, these bouquets were a money maker. When I finally left Bob, he said that I had SPONGED off him. I don't call what I did for the store as sponging.

A salesman working for an investment company came to the hamlet and sold Bob a retirement plan. I assumed that i would also be on the plan until the salesman said "Are you going to buy a plan for your wife, too?" Then I knew that Bob was only investing for himself and I was left on my own.

There was a dress shop on the main street. It was owned by a Mrs Wall who had borrowed money from our store to start her dress shop. She paid all the money back. Mrs. Wall ordered dresses in the sizes and colors that her customers liked and they bought them all. Then this dear lady died. She left a son and daughter and between them they got the proceeds from the dress shop and from her house. She had always worked very hard and was frugal. So these two offspring got quite a lot of money. Within six months they had squandered all the money that Mrs. Wall had worked so hard to make. Now the only place to purchase a dress was at the dry goods department store which was up the block and on the corner. This large store marked the end of the main street. The Scottish couple, although they owned the general store, also operated this department store. They lived upstairs and that was where they hosted the dinner parties. I liked going there because the food was always ample and good, even though quite rich.

The other buildings on the main street were the hotel next to our store, an automatic laundry, the only bank, an empty store, the general store, and a garage. There lived a little farther down on the main street, a family that had five strapping big boys and two girls. This family did something that I had never heard of. Each fall when their garden was done, they piled all the cabbages on the garden. When the cold weather came, the pile froze solid. When they wanted a cabbage, one of the boys would go out and chop one off the pile, take it in, and it would be good when cooked.

These boys must have had a consultation and a draw each fall to see who would court the new teacher who would be coming into the hamlet to teach. When the couple got married, all the boys in the family would pitch in and build a small house for them. The next year, the same thing. One year the draw must have been a super draw because one of them got the nurse. These boys, now men, treated their wives nicely and there was never a separation or a divorce. They were all good people. Since the senior family had the big garden and land around it, when the hamlet finally boomed they would be able to sell the property and get lots of money.

Since Bob was not buying me a retirement plan, I decided that I would get a job and buy my own plan. So I went to see the Sister Superior at the hospital to ask for work. What a shock I got. The hospital did not employ any nurses as they only ran the hospital with nuns who had been taught to do nurses' work. Here I was with all my education in nursing and no job. However, the Sister Superior said that she would hire me for periods when the sisters went on retreat, likely to the east to the mother ship, and that would be for two week periods once or twice a year.

At about the same time, a small house became available, a block away from Daniel and Lois's house and since we could not continue to live with them, we bought it. There was also a corner lot adjacent to the house and we bought that too. So I knew that I was stuck in the outpost hamlet.

This house had four rooms which consisted of two bedrooms, a living room, a kitchen, a back porch, and a front porch. The situation was much the same as the in laws house with a water barrel in the basement, a rain barrel outside, an oil floor furnace, an oil stove, a galvanized bath tub, and a chemical toilet. This toilet was in our bedroom so quite a bit of lime went in to it, again, to cut the odor. The contents of the chemical toilet were thrown on the garden at the back of the house. Bob made us a headboard for the bed, but didn't sand it or stain it, in other words, did not finish it but it did the job as I could put books on it, but it was not very pretty.

By this time we had our son and also a daughter. They both slept in the same bedroom in identical brown cribs, then in beds. There was also a potty chair in the room, but my son would not use it. He preferred droppings in his trousers. When he was three years old, I showed him what little water I had to rinse out his underwear. He seemed to get that message because he then smartened up.

The theatre sent out a show card each month, so we went to most of the shows. My son loved the movies so he spent all of his indoor time tearing up paper to make what he called "show tickets" and filled a small suitcase with these pieces. Meanwhile his sister played with Barbie dolls and had doll clothes in her little suitcase. We had a sandbox on the next lot and it was right outside my kitchen window so I could easily watch the children. Our children and neighbour children would sit for hours in it and play. I put some holes in cans so the sand could run out and they had fun stacking them to make castles.

One early evening after the store closed at eight p.m., several of us were standing on the dock at the river. My two children were there and they both had life jackets on. Suddenly my little girl, then two, fell into the water and was immediately swept under the dock by the tide. Bob did not have a life jacket on but he jumped into the water and went under the dock. I did not know it then, but he and his friends used to play under the dock and they knew where the logs holding the dock were and where you could get your breath. To my relief at the other end of the dock,

Bob appeared and was holding our daughter. She was not hurt. Bob had saved her, thank goodness.

In the wintertime, I had persuaded Bob to drain the rain barrel onto our garden to freeze to make a skating rink. We had some small stools in the house and they were perfect for new skaters to hang onto to learn to skate. Quite a few of the children in the town learned to skate on that rink. All of the children would come into my kitchen, skates on and all. It was a wonder that there was any linoleum untouched. One day I was in the basement with the door at the top of the stairs open. My little son came in from playing outside, saw the door open, climbed on one of the stools from the living room and locked the latch. I was still in the basement, locked down there and had to wait a long time until the children came back in. They were not stupid children but it took them a little thinking to realize that I was shut in below them. The door to the basement was in the back porch. It was a slatted door with a hook at the top. The door opened onto a landing and a worn wooden staircase led down to an earthen floor. There was one light bulb hanging from the ceiling. I was busy sorting through my trunks in that basement which was only under half of the house. The basement contained the floor furnace and the water barrel that was filled once a week by the man driving the water truck. There was a small window over the water barrel so that the water man could see how much water was in the barrel and there was a small spout through the wall so he could put the water into the barrel. The oil barrel was outside.

My son had a small tricycle and with his sister standing on the back, he would ride around in the small kitchen, into the living room, around the coffee table and back to the kitchen. Not once did he bump into walls or hurt the house. That house was old, but it still was what we had and it was comfortable.

A lady who came into the town with her husband had had nine years of Scottish dance lessons. When she started teaching Scottish dancing, I enrolled my two children. I knitted them each a pair of plaid socks and made them kilts. Lois bought a sporran for my son for the front of his kilt. They wore soft black dancing slippers that laced up over the socks and above the kilts wore white tops. I helped the children learn the steps by saying them out loud. "Point, behind, in front, behind". These directions were how they pointed their toes and moved their legs. When the school concert came, the two of them danced together and did a very nice highland fling. Soon the teacher was expecting a baby, and as she got bigger, she still danced. What a spectacle when she was about eight months along to see her doing the sword dance. After she had the baby, she stopped teaching so my children only learned the highland fling. They never got to try the sword dance.

FIVE

Bob wasn't too bad of a husband except that he worked such long hours and didn't take off the Wednesday afternoon that he could have spent with me. In the winter time, he taught me to curl and I was the lead on his team, except when I was pregnant. I could put a nice rock or two in front of the house where he wanted it. Walking home from the curling rink, we could usually see the northern lights dancing across the sky. The lights were always different sometimes even having purple in them as well as having lots of greens. In this hamlet, it was free to see the northern lights almost every night but years later tour companies charged you for a trip to see the lights, usually farther to the north.

We also went to a lot of shows. Then there were some dances. We loved to dance and we learned the twist, a new dance. Bob would spin me around when we jived.

But, in order to try to be funny, when someone else danced with me he would say things like "that's right, get her warmed up for me" and "she should have worked the streets, because she is active in bed". Did I ever hate remarks like that. They weren't funny at all and they hurt me.

When we went to the city, we stayed at my mother's house. We bought a low cot made of canvas and it had four metal legs. This cot was for the children to sleep on and they would lie feet to feet. The children learned to lie still on that cot because if they didn't keep still, the cot would roll them out onto the floor. We called it the "Tippy Cot". I had that cot for years. If ever I tried to sleep on it, the cot was very efficient at rolling me off. When my older son was grown up, he asked me what had happened to the tippy cot. I still had it then but eventually gave it away.

When my mother and I lived in the west end, I had suggested to her that if we moved in the city to the university district, she could rent out rooms to students. So she bought a house that had a nice basement room with a small gas fireplace and with an open kitchen adjoining. The student could come in through the door that was half way down the kitchen stairs. There was not a problem renting the room. In fact, she had a waiting list for students wanting a place to live.

Upstairs on the main floor, also, my mother had a boarder. Her name was Polly. Polly worked at a spa in the west part of the city and she mostly did electrolysis, mostly on the upper legs of dancers. When we were there, Bob would get up early in the morning and drive Polly to work. Then he would go again at the time she was to come home to give her a ride home. At the time, I should have paid more attention, but I didn't think much about it. After a year, Polly moved to a city more to the south of where we were.

When we were back in the north, Bob used to go to this southern city, supposedly to "conventions" or whatever they were. I was busy at home usually looking after the children so I didn't go and I didn't worry about his trip. Big mistake!

Later on, Bob used to go to curling bonspiels in other towns and again I didn't go. Another big mistake! I wasn't a suspicious person so I didn't worry about these outings that he had. He went to curl.

At this early time, some of the oil companies were trying to develop the oil sands. When some of the pilots didn't have much to do, they would come to my house and take me flying with them or take me to their boat to water ski behind it. I loved water skiing. These outings were not a romantic thing or I would not have gone. They were only a friendship thing and it put in their time for the day. When flying, the pilots would always fly close to the river because then they knew where they were. If they were over the bush, and there was lots of that, every tree looked the same and it was easy to get lost. When in the air, the pilot would often fly to the north. I could always see lots more muskeg, the same as what I had seen from the train when I first travelled to the north. I would usually see buffalo, also called bison, wandering aimlessly about the west side of the river. Later the buffalo were put into a very large park, but they still had lots of space to roam around. From the front window of the plane, I could see the next small northern hamlet, but we didn't land there. The wide river over which we were flying was getting wider as it went north to the arctic. As far as a person could see to each side were trees and more trees. Sometimes there would be a moose or a deer to see. If the animal was close to where we were flying, it could hear the noise of the plane and would take off as fast as it could. The pilot taking me out for the day, would always have me back home before the children came home from school. When we were flying, we often passed Albert who flew the bigger Norseman plane every day to deliver baggage and mail to the northern areas. Albert was a handsome man and he later married one of my friends. When he couldn't fly in the north any more, they moved to the lower mainland to the coast where he did some flying and also worked on the planes there and helped with the passengers, loading and unloading. While they lived in the northern town, they had a female dog called Duchess. When Duchess had her first heat all the dogs of the hamlet came calling. There were fights, howls, and lots of disturbance day and night. It wasn't long after that that the vet in the big city fixed Duchess, so she didn't have another heat and the dog friends didn't come.

Each year teachers, usually a married couple, would come to the school in the hamlet north of our town. Since there was not a road to that area, the teachers had to make a list of all the articles and food that they would need for the year. I often wondered how they figured out how much yeast or flour that they would need. Then their supplies would go to the area by boat that towed a barge behind.

The children at the school, where they taught, stayed at the school all week and went home for the weekends. When they came back on Monday morning, they had to be shown again how to use the flush toilets and to wash at the sinks. But for most of the morning the teachers had to treat their heads to make sure that they were free of lice.

Once a year, a nurse would come on the boat to that northern hamlet and would make her rounds. She found that there was a high amount of a disease that had to be treated with antibiotics. The adults and children usually slept in the same room so the children knew the facts of life at an early age. One boy had the infectious disease that many of the parents had. The boy said that he used to "do that" when he was seven, but didn't do "it" anymore. Once everyone was looked after, the nurse would leave on the returning boat.

Once in a while on a Sunday, Bob would take the children and me out into the bush to shoot rabbits. If it was winter time, I was always nervous that we would get stuck in the snow and out on the bush road. We would usually get one or two rabbits and I would make a baked dish that the local people made. It was called "Jug Rabbit", but I did not put the wine in it because of the children. The rabbit meat tasted like chicken.

The rabbits reproduced on a seven year cycle. If there were few rabbits, they did fine because they had enough food but as there became more and more rabbits, the food got eaten faster so there was less of it. Rabbits are good at reproducing. When seven years was about up, we noticed that the trees, especially the birch trees, had the bark stripped off the trunks as far up as any rabbit could stretch. We guessed that the bark was not enough to prevent starvation or maybe it was poisonous, but whatever it was killed them and the cycle started again for the next seven years.

In later years when my older son was grown, I gave him a shotgun that had been left for me when James died. I said "Now you can go out and shoot rabbits". He almost had a fit and said "Shoot rabbits? I FEED the rabbits that come into my yard". He also fed the deer that walked through his yard and said that the deer were always very careful where they stepped so as not to hurt the plants. They knew a good thing when they had it.

SIX

There were only two churches in the outpost hamlet. They were the Roman Catholic Church on which land was the church, a school, and the hospital that had the quarters for the priest, the brothers, and the nuns behind it, and the protestant church which was Anglican. The Anglican Church had a basement where we had wedding showers and baby showers and any other gatherings. At some of these meetings the minister's wife would talk about her husband. The talk was not hurtful, but it was very funny. She knew a side to him that we didn't see. When this couple got to the hamlet, the minister's wife thought that the rectory where they lived had to be painted inside. That would have cost the church ladies a lot of money so we suggested that she get it washed first. After it was washed, it was perfect and didn't need a new paint job. The minister's wife asked me if I would make her a dress. I agreed. So I ordered some material and some lining to make her a nice dress. The material was royal blue with flowers on it. When I started to measure the woman, I realized that she had a hump on her back. I had to work quite hard to fit the back of the dress over the hump. However, the dress fit her nicely and she said it was the nicest dress that she had ever had. I was glad that she was happy with it.

At these gatherings, there was always a game or a quiz. I had to stop writing down the answers because I always won. I was the only one with a university education. There was always a big lunch and I took meat sandwiches made with meat, pickle and dressing mixed together and they were always all eaten. The meat that I used came out of a can and was the popular canned meat in the north.

At Christmas time there was always a concert in this basement. When my son was a little over three years old, he was on the stage with his younger sister and a group of children. The children on the stage wondered why some of the people in the audience were giggling while they were singing. My son was singing his heart out but at the same time was zipping the fly on his pants up and down. He never realized what he was doing but it was very funny.

The ladies in the group that raised money to keep the church in good repair were only four in number. There was the wife of the general store manager, the bank manager's wife, a wife whose husband worked for the government, and myself. We raised money throughout the year to pay for any needs for the church and rectory. Some of the money maker ideas that we did were to make Christmas cakes at Christmas time and sell them. Then we decided that we could also sell Christmas puddings, so our customers bought both. The baking was done at my house with the oil stove, which had taken me quite a while to master. We also had a vacant shop lent to us rent free and we operated a thrift store there every Saturday. People gave us a lot of things to sell because we were closer than the dump, but lots of other people came to buy. The shop was popular and was profitable.

We decided that we could make some money if we put on a fashion show and charged admission. The show was to be on the stage at the theatre. I knew that my cousin who was older than I was had a trunk full of clothes from the 1920's. I had been her flower girl at her wedding many years before. Her husband also had a trunk full but it was full of ribbons from winning with his purebred Belgian horse at the Canadian National Exhibition in Toronto. When that horse was home, we were forbidden to go anywhere near to his coral, because he was so high bred and high strung that my cousin said he would break the coral apart if we bothered him. But he was a prize winner.

So I contacted my cousin about the clothes so she boxed them up and sent them on the train. Also, the department store lent us new clothes and we got some of the school children to model them. We didn't know much about modeling, but we taught our models how we thought they should walk and turn on the stage.

When I got on the stage, I had on a thin dress from the early days and a stylish hat that my mother had worn long ago. The audience started to whistle, clap, and cheer. I didn't know why I was getting such a reception but I later found out that with the lighting that was on, the patrons could see right through my dress to my legs and my underclothes. I don't know if that was why the show was so successful or not, but we did make money. Bob was mad at me and would have preferred me to have worn a heavy coat on the stage.

The lady in our little group who was the wife of a government worker, was a little different. She had five children and ironed absolutely everything in the house, even the socks. She played the organ faithfully in the church every Sunday. Not many people attended church. and not Bob. The Scottish man was there every Sunday and he put five dollars in the collection plate each week. That was a lot of money in those days. The bank manager's wife and I occasionally sang together in the church because she was used to singing with her several sisters but they didn't live in the outpost hamlet so I was the singing partner.

One day when the minister was downtown at the bank, the bank manager asked him why the church women didn't have much money in their account. So the minister went to the head of our group who owned and worked at the general store and together they examined the account. What had happened was that the treasurer who played the organ in the church each Sunday, had spent the money at the department store, small cheque by small cheque. In other words, she had used most of the money and her husband now had to pay it back. We were surprised at her but we kept it all quiet. She still remained in our group as the treasurer and she still played the organ in the church every Sunday as if nothing had happened. If we had not kept it quiet, she might have been put in jail and who would look after her children or her husband. He certainly would not iron the socks.

Across the street from our house was a big square house that was the police barracks for the one policeman in the town. The offices were on the main floor, the cells were in the basement, and the family lived upstairs. The policeman's wife had grown up in a large family that had been poor. They rarely got cake to eat, but when they did there never was any icing on it. So this woman was ravenous for sweets. When we had a "do", she never ate any sandwiches, just sweets. Her husband, the policeman, was also from a big family. He was the oldest of eleven children, and when he was young and went downtown or anywhere else, people would stare at him because his mother was always pregnant. He couldn't do anything about it. He managed to save up enough money to take police training to become a policeman. When he graduated from the school and could wear the police uniform he always was proud and was a good policeman.

His wife, Sonja, knew that I used clippers to cut Bob's and my son's hair. So she too ordered some clippers from Eaton's catalogue. Her first haircut was on her husband.

The policeman came to my door to ask if I could do anything about his hair. Talk about a haircut done with a bowl on top. That was it! I told him "yes, I can fix it but you will have a short haircut." So I gave him a crew cut. The man felt badly that his wife did not give him a nice haircut. I could see the pain in his face. So I told him to go home, put on his dress uniform and look in the mirror so that he would see himself as the policeman with a fairly good crew cut. Then he should feel better.

The policeman asked me if I would babysit a woman prisoner that he had in a cell in the basement. The job would be at night and I would be paid. So I took the job. This woman was a tough cookie. I had to open her cell to give her coffee, food, and to take her to the bathroom. She must have known that I was afraid of her because she wanted something about every 15 minutes. The bathroom trips were the worst because she was free to walk. She didn't escape but I didn't like this job and didn't work for the policeman again.

One of the things, among many, that I didn't like about the hamlet was that Bob and I would get to be friends with the bank manager and wife, but, in about two years, they would be transferred out to another town. I tried to contact some of these people when we were in the city, but because they were bank people, they kept much to themselves. One of the couples who had been in the northern area usually had their house so untidy that it looked like a cyclone had hit it, but when the parents with the children stepped outside, they looked like they had been turned out by a beauty shop. The wife of another couple who came there was so unhappy with the suite above the bank that she made the bank big wigs redo it all and put in all new appliances. The suite above the bank had a spy hole in the floor where the bank manager could watch a thief take money. The hole could also be used to look down onto a teller who was well endowed on the top. Her "top" would be over the desk. The men of the town loved to go to the bank to see the "top" of this teller. Otherwise, the hole was not much help unless the manager wanted to apprehend the thief, which I'm sure he wouldn't want to do, and he could not interfere with the teller because she was single and he had a wife.

When I was in nursing school, we were taught that if someone from outside the hospital wanted to apprehend us to steal medicines or the narcotics, we were to give them the keys to the locked cupboard and say "Hop to it". The narcotics were not worth much, but our lives were worth more.

SEVEN

The hospital was an outpost hospital and was classed as "F". There were nineteen beds which included four cots for newborns and six cribs for toddlers. On the main floor was a private room, a corner for the dumb waiter, the nurses' station, three beds in one ward, a room with the six cribs for the toddlers and the examining room which had the autoclave in an alcove at the back. The upstairs had a private room, the corner for the dumb waiter, a room for the newborn babies, a cupboard for the narcotics and the medicines, a room for the maternity ward, a small kitchenette where we could mix formula, and the case room. The stairs to the second floor had a turn in them so if a patient had to be carried downstairs, the post at the turn could be removed. There was not a stretcher or a wheelchair in the whole place so when a woman was in labor and was about to deliver, we had to wait between contractions and WALK the woman to the delivery table. The case room was always set up so all that had to be done was to open the sterile bundles and add any fluids or sutures. Sometimes when a woman was having trouble pushing out the baby, the doctor made push on the upper part of the abdomen in order to give extra pressure. I thought that this was very strange because we were never taught to do that in nursing school but the old doctor had delivered lots of babies and there was not an operating room within miles to get a C section done.

The other thing that I thought was strange was when a newborn baby needed fluid, the sister showed me how to inject fluid into the back of the baby at each side of the spine until the fluid bump was the size of one of my fingers. Luckily, I never had to do this. I'm sure that such a bump hurt.

When I worked the night shift, there were some chores that I had to do. I had to set up a little altar in the hall on the second floor so there was a place for some of the patients to pray. At about four a.m, I also had to measure out the porridge for the morning and put the ingredients into a big pot and put it on the back of the stove. The porridge would simmer away and be ready for the morning breakfast for the brothers and sisters. The Sister Superior gave me the keys to the store room that was like a big pantry. She said for me to help myself and take anything that I wanted to eat. I looked into the room, didn't take anything, but did see a whole row of salt-peter. I didn't put any into the porridge, but I guess it went into the food periodically to quiet the urges of the brothers and sisters.

There was a beautiful young girl who cleaned the rooms for the priest and the brothers. It wasn't long before she had two small children. They had the same father because they both looked alike. After that, she was well looked after and so were the children. They had nice clothes and money to spend.

The nurse on duty, when not busy, sat in the office on the main floor. Each morning, one of the sisters came down, got on the scale that was in our nursing office where we sat when we were not busy, and said "Oh, oh! Gaining weight again." At the same time, she was furiously knitting baby clothes. A few months later she wasn't there and I asked where she was. I was told that she was on retreat in the east. After a time she was back, minus the weight and minus the baby clothes. There hadn't been enough salt- peter used for her.

In the summertime on a Friday morning, you could often see two or the nuns in a boat on a nearby lake. They were fishing for fish for the priest, the brothers, the sisters, and the hospital patients for Friday night's fish supper. But, they were net fishing which was illegal. The policeman could not arrest two nuns because they were known to be good people, so as he would drive by, he would just wave at them and pretend that he didn't know what they were doing.

There was a vestibule along the hall to the sisters' quarters. Each afternoon at 2 p.m. the sisters had reading period in that area. They sat in a semi circle and each of them had a book but not a novel of course. As I would pass, I never saw anyone turn a page and two of them had their books upside down. I think that they all enjoyed that time, because they were resting and dreaming.

The sister who was next in line below the Sister Superior must have had a racy life before she had become a nun. If you wanted to know anything about the facts of life, you could ask her. She knew it all. It was hard to realize that the nuns had all had a life before they came to their calling. They were all so sweet and polished.

Part of my job on the night shift was to ring the bell to wake up the brothers and sisters. If I was busy, I couldn't ring the bell very early. So when the sisters came out of their rooms in the morning, they were all smiling because they had been able to sleep in.

One night I had treated two men who had come to the hospital from one of the camps. I was saying goodbye to them when they were walking to their truck. I was half way out of the door, and the door slipped out of my hand. I was then locked out of the hospital. I could not ring the bell to bring my helper downstairs because it would wake up the priest and all the brothers and sisters. The temperature was fifty five below and I only had on a cotton uniform and nylon stockings. So I hurried to the truck and told the men not to drive away until I got back into the hospital. I would have had to sit with them in their truck so as not to freeze to death. My helper had not come downstairs when I rattled the door because she knew that I was down there. Finally she peaked down the stairs and saw me outside and let me in.

Everything happened at that hospital. One night I smelled some smoke, so I ran around to see what was burning. I found a waste basket with something in the bottom smoldering. I grabbed the waste basket which wasn't yet hot, and threw it out the front door. This time I didn't let go of the door.

Another night, I was sitting in the downstairs office and something told me to check the newborns in the nursery upstairs. When I got there, I was horrified to see one of the babies turning purple. So I grabbed the baby by the feet and ran down the hall to where the only suction machine was in the case room. When I put the baby on the table, she was nice and pink. The jiggling of her as I ran down the hall had dislodged the mucous and she was now fine. She was the newborn of one of my friends and I would not have been happy to tell the mother that her baby had choked. We also had to be careful that the newborns were not bleeding from their umbilical cord, because one of the doctors tied the cord with only string which was not as good as a clamp. He later came around and used clamps which did a good job.

In the toddler's nursery on the main floor, there was a cookie jar with arrowroot biscuits in it. Every day, one of the nuns would come into that nursery, and say "kitchy-kitchy-coo" to each toddler and give every child a cookie. Sometimes a second nun would come in and the same thing would be repeated. More cookies! All of the children would then have diarrhoea. The day nurse and I tried to hide the cookie jar but to no avail. The nuns would snoop around and get the cookie jar out again. As a last resort, we threw the cookie jar away, but we still had a lot of diarrhoea because before any big do in the hamlet, some of the people would feed their children a lot of blueberries. Then the children would be making a mess in their diapers and the parents would bring them to the hospital. This was free babysitting service so that the parents could go to the gala. We knew what was happening but couldn't do anything about it as we had to look after the children. The blueberries gave grand diarrhoea which had to be cured.

One night when I came to work, i learned that there had been a bus accident on the highway. All of the passengers had had to come to the hospital to be treated. They were by then all looked after and were gone, but the hospital was a shambles. Every wrapped bundle had been used. All of the articles from the bundles had been washed but had to be sterilized. I spent the entire night sorting, wrapping, and autoclaving. We had to have the hospital ready for the next emergency or for a maternity patient coming in. Luckily we never had two maternity patients needing the case room for delivery at the same time. The sisters were quite smart about making things for the outpost so we also made and sterilized our own vaseline gauze and pads for hemorrhoids. Everything was useful. Even tiny caps off medicine bottles were taken to the school and the younger children planted a seed in them.

We sometimes had some unusual patients. A maternity patient delivered twins, but only had one breast that was usable for feeding. She fed both babies on the one side. The Sister Superior said for us to leave her alone, that the patient would figure it out. We thought that maybe she had a friend at home who was weaning a baby so she would be able to have her feed one.

Then we had as a patient a woman who was very prominent in the hamlet. She was the most prim and proper person that you would ever know. But, when we had her, she would take her cane and hit the patient in the next bed. Another patient that we had, had sores on his lower abdomen. The doctor had ordered us to put compresses on them. Luckily, we were using forceps to put the compresses on. We asked the doctor several times if he would do a blood test on this fellow. Finally he agreed and when the results came back they were extremely positive. So, that was enough of the compresses and the patient was put on antibiotics. If we had not have urged for the test, the man later on would have lost his mind and be untreatable. Beethoven had the same disease.

One night, I was doing a dressing on the abdomen of a male patient. The sheet over his lower abdomen kept coming up towards my sterile field. I kept pushing the sheet back down. Then I realized that what I was pushing was more than just the sheet. That patient had a big grin on his face. He thought that he was in heaven with an angel working on him.

Sometimes people would come to the hospital to speak with the Sister Superior to get work. She would hire them but know that they were not registered nurses. They would be paid less money than educated nurses. One young lady said that she had been in Germany in the war and that her papers had been destroyed. She did know something about hospital work, but spent all of her spare time in our office reading the book of questions and answers that covered registered nursing exams. From the dumb questions that this worker asked me, I knew that she had never had nurses' education. The other day nurse and I did not have to read that book because we knew our work. At the hospital where I graduated, we had to write New York state board exams for our final tests. These exams meant that we could go to any hospital in the world and not have to take any course to work there. One nurse in our class only got one halfway through these exams and was sure that she had failed, but all of her answers must have been correct because she passed with the rest of us. I won an operating room prize but never worked in an operating room after that although I had to help deliver lots of babies.

When this hospital worker who had "lost" her papers left the town to go elsewhere, the Sister Superior refused to give her a reference letter and also said that if anyone enquired about her she would deny that she had ever worked there. The Sister Superior was a very smart person.

The next person who came to work at the outpost hospital was also from Germany. Her name was Lizzy. All of Lizzy's family had been killed in the concentration camps. Lizzy was a big strong woman and fast figured out that if she worked hard for the guards, she would get ample bread and broth for the evening hand out. First, she set ties on the railway by working along with the men. This railway was needed to bring loads of people into the camps that had the gas chambers. After a time, Lizzy got moved into a hospital setting where the Germans were doing experiments on people. That is where Lizzy learned about hospital work. She worked hard in order to survive. There were lots of things that Lizzy would not talk about because it was too painful for her. She especially would not tell about the experiments that the Germans had been doing. Lizzy was quite excitable and when a maternity patient would come to the door and she was alone on duty at night, she would holler "maternity patient in the front hall". This hollering in the middle of the night would wake up all of the sleepers in the sisters and brothers quarters.

Lizzy liked me especially when she got sick with bad runs. I helped her back to health by feeding her distilled water first, then peach juice and dry toast next. As a result of me helping her, she gave me a beautiful vase that was eighty years old. I still have it and it is much older now. When I had it appraised quite some time ago, it was worth a lot of money.

After Lizzy left, there came to the hospital a woman looking for work. She did have some nurses training but was not licensed. The narcotics were in a small room that contained shelves with all the medicines on them. The narcotic cupboard was locked and these drugs were counted at each change of shift but there were many drugs that were not counted. On one of the shelves in the room was a jar of 222's. These pills could be given out as needed to patients for pain and they were not part of the narcotic count. Each pill contained one eighth of a grain of codeine, so if you took two, you would get one quarter of a grain of codeine.

Since the day registered nurse and I were in charge of the medicines and pills, I had to tell the Sister Superior that I thought that the jar of 222's was going down. No patients were getting them. So the nuns started counting the pills in this jar, and, yes, they were decreasing in number. So early one morning, the nuns counted the pills. When this worker had worked a few hours, they counted the pills again. Then they knew what was happening. There were already fewer 222's in the jar.

At one p.m., the policeman came to the hospital and arrested this worker. She was stealing narcotics and this was a very serious offence. It didn't matter that the pills only had a certain amount of narcotics in them, this crime was as bad as if they had been hard street drugs. When this woman was convicted if she got out of a life sentence, she would be lucky.

EIGHT

For two summers when I had been at university, I had worked for the police. I had been able to ride in a police car with various policemen. I learned what to say to a couple who were having a marital dispute, how to do a stake out, not to put my eye to a spy hole in a door in case I got shot through the hole, and which shop had the best donuts.

Because I worked a lot of night shifts, I sometimes had trouble sleeping. One night, when it was late, I was sitting on our front porch, and I saw Big Tom coming up my street. Big Tom lived as a squatter in a house down by the river. The house was now only a shack. Big Tom was staggering and was swinging what looked like a machete. I watched him go past, go downtown, and head for the hotel. Perhaps he was looking for trouble.

In the morning when Bob went to work early, he saw a lump beside the hotel and it was on the side facing our store. He went over to look. The area was muddy so Bob left footprints in the mud with his extra large boots. Then he picked up the machete to look at it. So here were Bob's big footprints on the ground and his fingerprints on the knife.

Not long afterwards, Bob was arrested and put into a cell which was in the police barracks across from our house. So I had to go to the policeman to tell him what I had seen of Big Tom staggering down the street with the machete and that Bob had been home asleep in bed. Big Tom was found asleep in the stairwell behind the theatre. When Big Tom was questioned, he admitted that he had met the person that he didn't like but had only meant to scare him. The knife had slipped and accidentally killed his enemy. He also admitted to being quite drunk which at that time was a good excuse to get released. So Big Tom was not charged and Bob was released from the cell. Bob was ever so thankful that he had not been charged with murder. He also learned not to mess with a crime scene. The yellow tape was taken from around the hotel when the body was removed and everything was back to normal.

NINE

When Christmas was nearing, I asked Bob if we could have a stand up dinner buffet at our house. He agreed and thought that it would be good advertizing for the store. Everything that he thought about was so that the store would make money. That money would eventually be his.

So we invited quite a lot of people who were our friends. I borrowed from a restaurant in town, a big wok that was three feet in diameter and I made it full of chow mein. I also made cakes and jellied foods that could be made the day before or frozen. We could even freeze items on the front porch where it was well below zero. We also cut up turkey that we had ordered from my cousins' farm. When we ordered the turkeys from my relatives we would tell them "the bigger the better". The relatives liked us taking all the biggest turkeys, some 48 pounds in weight, as the city people only wanted small turkeys and the city is where they sold most of them. So my relations were happy with us because we would order twelve turkeys each fall. We had a big, big roaster that could contain such a large turkey to cook it. So with a lot of turkey and all the food that I made, there was ample food.

When the day close to Christmas came, I got several phone calls from friends who had been invited. These people had had company from the big city come to visit them and they wanted to bring them to the party. So the guest list got longer and longer until it was over forty five people. That number of people in our small house was a lot of guests.

There was only standing room in the small house but everyone had a good time and had lots to eat. When they left, the wok on the stove was empty and so were most of the dishes on the table.

If it was not fishing season when we would go for a picnic, we would be invited every Sunday to the inlaw's house for dinner. In a way it was good because I got a holiday from cooking, but it was so boring for me. Bob was glued to his parents, especially his mother. He loved being there.

Almost each morning, one of his parents would walk into our house and be in my kitchen almost before I could get organized for the day.

I had been told before I had married Bob, that we would be in the outpost hamlet for one year. How gullible I was at that time. Here we were, going on to ten years, and no sign that we were ever going back to the big city.

I was thinking more and more about taking the children and leaving Bob. He would go away for lots of weekends, supposedly to go on buying trips or to go to curling bonspiels.

One weekend when he went away to a bonspiel, I saw the "third" of his curling team (Bob was the skip), still in town. There could not be a bonspiel out of town or I would not have seen this "third". I then knew that he wasn't where he said he was. I was home with the children and was waiting to get a phone call from him to say when he would be home. But I did not hear from him. Instead, I got a call from his mother who told me that Bob had said for her to call me and tell me that he would be home on Monday. That was the limit! He had phoned his MOTHER! I knew now that he had not phoned me because he must have had a guilty conscience about what he had been doing that weekend. Since there was not a bonspiel, he might have been visiting in the southern city where Polly worked, but I was just guessing. However, that was when I made up my mind to leave the guilty husband. No question about it.

So I told the Sister Superior at work that I was leaving and not to talk about it. For the next few days, I packed up some things for myself and the children. There were a few people in the town that I could trust and one of them drove me with my children to the train. Bob had left money on the counter at home so I could buy the groceries, but I just left it there. He still considered that I sponged off him.

I did not stop in the city to see my mother because she considered that the smooth talking Bob was a prince and so she would try to get me to go back. She didn't know that the "prince" was friendly with her former boarder.

The next train took me almost to the coast. The children loved the trip because they got to sleep in a bunk on the train and had a porter who entertained them. We went to stay with some friends who lived near to the city. I needed a job, so I phoned to the nurse registry to see where there was work. The person answering told me not to try the city hospitals as they were all full but that there was a job at Hope and a job at Squamish. I picked Squamish because it was closer. When I phoned there, I was asked to start immediately.

By that time, my friend, Sam, who had loaded me onto the train in the northern town, decided that if I could have enough courage to leave the hamlet, so could he. His marriage had been in trouble for a long time. So, as my friend, he came to where I was. That was good because he came in his car and I didn't have one. We loaded some furniture lent to us, went to Squamish, and rented a half of a duplex. I put the children into the school and started my job. Sam got a job with a local electric company.

The company that he worked for was doing electrical work at Alta Lake, to the north. If he had taken me there to see the country, I would have seen the potential and would have bought a couple of vacant lots that were at that time, very cheap. That area nearby later became Whistler. But I didn't get there so I missed out on what would have been a lucrative investment.

When Sam was downtown one day, he saw Bob driving a rental car with my two children in the back and they were waving at him. So I had to get a city lawyer and then there was a court case about my children. That province was loaded with welfare children at that time, and the court did not want my children to join the crowd. So the court result was decided before the case was heard. It was kangaroo court. During the case, Bob said that his mother would quit work and look after the children. They believed him and he and the children were sent back to the outpost town. She never did look after them but kept working in the store. The children had a baby sitter. I didn't go back with them because if I had, I knew that Bob would treat me like a naughty child. Bob had found out where the children were living because when the request for our children's records was made by the northern school, the principal of the school where the children were, broke his confidentiality oath and told smooth talking Bob where we were. Squamish!

In a few months, I wanted to see our children. So I took a plane trip to the northern town. As I got off the plane, the taxi driver that I was about to hire to take me down the hill to the town, was on the phone. I assumed that he was phoning Bob to squeal that I was in town. He didn't gain much, because a few weeks later, he had an accident on the highway and was killed.

When I got to the house, the young baby sitter had the children inside and would not let me see them, but the children were peaking out the windows. So this was a wasted trip.

A few months later, I made another trip to see them, but this time I had a court order from the city judge that I was to take them on a holiday. I got them then and we had a nice time. The next trip was to be a meeting in the city, but on the way out of the town, Bob had an accident with the car and scooted back to the town and to his mother.

By this time, I had married Sam and we had a girl child. I thought that it was not fair to her to keep trying to see the other children in the north. So I gave up on them. When my boy grew up, he told me that that was the best thing that I did was to stop trying to visit them because it made their lives easier when I did not come.

At Squamish, the air from Woodfibre, across the bay, was bothering my chest. So I phoned to Kamloops hospital and they hired me. I had asked for the maternity ward, but that was full so I was put on the medical ward. I hated it there. Before we could do any work on our shift, we had to check all medicine cards against the kardex (like a file folder), and check the kardex against the doctors' orders. Didn't the powers in charge trust anyone? So after about an hour of this checking we could start work.

On the medical ward were two chronic patients who had been medically addicted to drugs. I had them both. They would get there drugs that could only be given every four hours and in two and a half hours, they would start hollering for the next dose that couldn't be given until the time was up. This was very upsetting for me. The doctor who had allowed them to become addicted never should have kept chronic patients on narcotics. We were the ones who suffered and these patients suffered too. One early morning when this doctor was driving home, he went to sleep at the wheel, went over the bank, and drowned in the river.

I just about got fired from that hospital because I had come out of the north where we did what was needed. We also had to be the doctor when he was out of town. So on this one shift, I had given a patient a laxative but without a doctor's order. My! My! It was only laxative. Another time I was hurrying down the hall with an enema can and some lubricant in my hand, and the nurse manager asked me what I was doing. She could see what the enema can was for, but she made me go back to the service room and set everything on a tray with a cloth cover on the tray and a cover over the top. She stood there and watched me. What a waste of time! In the north, the maternity patients all needed an enema and sometimes we had to rush because they were about to deliver the baby. We just needed the can and the goop. We couldn't set up an enema tray there because we didn't have one or any cloth to go on it. No wonder the hospital was a class "F". It didn't have an enema tray or any cloths for it! We could have used a meal tray but that would not have been too nice for the next patient with their meal on that tray.

One day on that medical ward, I had a male patient who was the cook on a big, big ranch that had lots of cattle. I knew of the family and the ranch and they were rich. As part of my work, I was keeping track of this patient's fluid tally and had my paper and pen on the side table. My pen was a good fountain pen and had my name engraved on it. The pen went missing. The next day, I made such a fuss about my pen, that soon the pen was back. They had stolen it and they knew that I knew that they had taken it. The following day, I asked for another patient and my pen was safely in my pocket.

In Kamloops we lived in a quite good apartment up the hill from the hospital. I had to walk up the hill in the heat to get home. On my day off one day, the washer was not being used. This day was not my day to use the washer, but since it wasn't being used I slipped a small load into it. Out of one of the doors came a woman who was yelling at me that it was her day for the washer. After my load was done, she didn't use the washer and not at all on that day. That was my experience in that expensive apartment.

Sam was soon out of work because he had worked for six months and had been promised a bonus after six months. Kamloops was one of the first stops for men from the prairies who would arrive and ask for work. So it was cheaper to take a newcomer than to give someone who had worked six months a wage increase as promised. So Sam was let go. At each place where we lived we were not happy with the houses there, so since I had some money and Sam knew how to build, we built a house. But, when work gave out, we would have to sell the house unfinished. Sam went farther north than Kamloops to get another job. I was living in the house until it was sold. On the day that the man buying it paid the money to the lawyer, he was at my door to get the key and move in. I had a hard job explaining to him that he did not get possession until the actual closing date and I was still entitled to live there. By this time I had my baby daughter. From this northern city, we had to move again and we went to Williams Lake. There we started a store for Sam to look after. Sam didn't like staying in the store so he would sit in the coffee shop across the street. Then the young clerk quit. When we checked the store and the extra stock in the back room, all of the boxes there were empty. She had taken all of what was in the boxes. We didn't have any proof against her so we just lost out. Her next job was in a bank. Good luck to them!

I had been working the night shift in the hospital and one morning when I was walking home, I heard a noise like a cat behind a snow bank. When I looked, I saw a little child with only a wet diaper on. She was partly blue, so I picked her up, wrapped her in my coat, went home, put some of my child's clothes on her and called the police. The police said "We don't want her". So I explained to them that I didn't want to be accused of kidnapping this child. I had to sleep after my night shift, so I took the child back to the apartment building and asked a woman in one of the apartments if she would keep the child and I would come back in the afternoon. When I went back, this woman had found the mother who had been asleep when the child went out. The problem was solved.

We did not fit in at that city because most of the people rode a horse. Also, a lot of them were heavy drinkers. We didn't do those things, so Sam arranged a job to repair appliances in the lower mainland and we prepared to move. This time we bought a house. When it was time to leave and move into that house, the real estate man told us that the people in the house were not out yet, but that they had cleared a bedroom where we could live for a time and have our things there. Our "things" were a whole house of furniture including a piano and a dog. Because the dog saw the boxes getting packed, he worried so much that when we got there, he was bleeding. I figured that he had gotten an ulcer. So I fed him only milk for a week and he was better.

The people from whom we were buying the house finally cleared out because I told them that my truckers that were coming would not unload any of my goods until the house was empty. The real estate man tried to tell me that that was how it was done in that city and that the people could not get a truck. I wasn't swallowing any of that and told them that there were lots of truckers looking for work.

When I was having a bath one day, my small daughter came into the bathroom, looked at herself in the mirror and said," Mommy, am I going to die?" I don't know what she had seen in the mirror but I replied," I hope not".

We had bought a lot to build one more house. When I would drive my daughter up to the lot to look at it, she never wanted to go and would scream at me. It was before Valentine's Day so my little girl got busy and made valentines and delivered them early to all her friends on the street.

The next Sunday after church, we drove to the lot to do a little tidying up. Sam told our daughter to take the dogs and sit on the log at the back of the lot. She did that for a little while and then moved forward while at the same time, Sam felled a tree. The tree landed on her and broke her neck. She was only six years old. I took one look and knew that she was dead. I ran to the nearest house, burst in their front door, shouted out that my husband had cut down a tree that fell on our daughter and I collapsed on their inside steps. I was in shock. When I woke up, I was in the emergency room at the hospital and the doctor said that our daughter was dead. She was buried in a dress that I had bought for her and when I had taken the dress home, I said that it looked like an angel's dress. Now she was going with the angels and in that dress.

I mourned for my daughter for a year. Sam did not mourn at all and friends said that he would have repercussions much later. After a while, we contacted the welfare and asked for a child. The lady in charge came several times to our house to check us out. Every time before she came, I would gather up any newspapers or other items out of place and put them in the dryer. Then she said that she had a boy for us but was giving us his medical papers to take to our doctor. Normally they did not give out medical papers. Our doctor took one look at the papers and said "You're not having this child. You will spend all of your life taking him to psychiatrists in the big city to try to help him." We were not the first set of approved parents who refused this child. I was smart enough to realize that the welfare would never offer us another child, even though they had lots of them.

So I phoned an obstetrician that I knew in another town, told him what had happened and asked him if he would give us a baby. He said "We'll see". A few months later he phoned us and said "I have the girl". We waited and waited. Then, at four a.m. one night he phoned and said "You have a son". We were at that hospital the next day, but could not take our son until the fourth day because he had to be under a bili light since he had had some jaundice. On the fourth day, the doctor carried our son out of the hospital and put him in my arms. The welfare lady saw us once after that but couldn't do anything because it was a private adoption. The papers were all done in the city where he was born and he was ours. I had promised the delivery doctor that I would work hard to be sure that this boy was cared for and got educated. He ended up with a master's degree.

A year or so later Sam started to get different which, I believe, was from him not ever grieving over our daughter's death. He was picking on me all the time and got in his head four delusions. Delusions are ideas that are not based on fact. Two of the delusions that he had were that I was sleeping with various men and that I was stealing money. If the hospital where I worked heard about these delusions, I would at least be disciplined if not fired.

One day a neighbour across the street called me over and said" You should hear what your close neighbour is saying about you". I said "You don't have to tell me because I know". Somehow I had to stop this neighbour that lived close to my house, from spreading Sam's delusions. So I invited her in for tea. After we had the tea, I said "I know what you have been saying around the neighbourhood about me and I want you to know that by law I am protected from slander". She could have said" What are you talking about?", but instead she jumped to her feet and said "I don't have to take this". I replied "No, you don't" and she stomped out of my house. But this put a stop to her and my husband's delusions that she was spreading around the neighbourhood, delusions that were not true.

Sam was still picking on me so that I felt like a worm on the ground. One day he raised his arm to hit me so I got the Sherriff to put him out of the house. He was gone a few days when he sweet talked me into letting him back home. He hadn't changed. His behavior was the same so I put him out again. A few days later a man came to the house and handed me some papers. The papers were an affidavit of eleven pages of lies about me. I took all the papers to the lawyer and asked him what kind of a case it would be to refute these lies. The lawyer said that this was a big case and that we would have to get psychiatrists from the city to testify on my behalf. He also said that when we won, Sam would do the case again, and the third time the judge would say that it was enough. Total time would be about six years. I knew that I could not work six years to win a case and work at my job as well. So I signed over my son to Sam but asked to get very good visiting rights.

Next thing, the dog went missing. I knew that Sam had taken him so I went down the street to the apartment where his boss had told me Sam with my son was living. I stayed on the sidewalk and as loud as I could, I called the dog. I did this for two days. I really made a racket. On the third day the dog was home. The dog had heard me for sure and I knew that the apartment owner had had a part in getting that dog out because he had to stop me yelling in front of his building.

Sam's boss who was helping me, told me that Sam had moved with my son to the next town, but that he didn't know where they were. So I went to that town, went up and down the streets until I found his vehicle. Often when I would go to pick up my son for the visiting, Sam would not be there. He thought of lots of tricks to make things difficult for me.

Next Sam transferred to Nanaimo. Now, I had to take the ferry, then the taxi, to pick up our son, and then taxi back to the ferry. If I was lucky, we could get back onto the same ferry. One day when I went up to Sam's house, there was a note on the door that said "Be back soon". So I waited on the vacant lot next door. When noon came and I was still waiting, I ran the two blocks down the hill to the store and bought some food. Sam had not come home yet. I had waited all day. Soon it was time for me to catch the last ferry to the mainland so I again went to the store, got a taxi and went to the ferry. Sam had won that day big time.

Then one of the taxi drivers told me that their company took children by themselves all over the city. He said to phone them when the ferry was coming in and they would go to the house and bring my son down to the ferry. I had to arrange with Sam for this transport by the taxi. He finally agreed to the arrangement but didn't want to make it that easy for me.

Then Sam was going to get remarried. I almost went to see his fiance, whom I knew, to tell her to take more time before she got married but I thought that she would consider it sour grapes on my part. Later, when she was getting a divorce, she told me that she wished that I had warned her. They moved now into the United States into a coast home that Sam and I had built. In our divorce, Sam had gotten this home and I gotten the home in the city where I worked. They were living in the U.S. illegally.

This lady was very nice to our son, but Sam was treating her the same way that he had treated me. He was Mr. Smooth talker when company was there but when they were alone, he was abusive and demanding. When she got to that house, she had put under the bed a box with papers in it. The papers were about a piece of property that she was buying and she had two more payments to make on it. Just like my dog, the box disappeared. She didn't know in her head the legal number of the property so she couldn't go to the land titles office to check on it. She never got the box back and never got the property.

She lasted with Sam for almost five years, then got a divorce. When she was still with him, she phoned me to tell me that Sam was planning to move to Nova Scotia where he had been stationed in the war. With that move, I almost never would be able to see my son. So I went back to the court and got him restricted to the two western provinces. He was furious. I had foiled his plotting.

Then, the next move that he made was to the other province, quite a distance for me to go but I went as often as I could. I wanted to try to help my son grow up to be a decent person, a good husband, and a good father. He became all of that and he has been a blessing to me.

TEN

I was doing a home business besides working at the hospital and with the money that I had made, I bought my son a new truck in order for him to have transportation to university. He came to the province where I was and drove the truck home. I had gotten him a truck because I didn't want him having seating space to transport a bunch of young people around. Next thing that I knew, he had listened to his peers and had traded that new truck for a nine year old sedan. The dealer that made the agreement with him must have laughed until he couldn't laugh anymore.

When it was time for university, Sam got him enrolled at the satellite college a little way out of the city. He asked me to pay the tuition fees which I gladly did because I had promised the obstetrician who had delivered him that the baby would get educated and never be without. Our son was at that college for two years and for the two years that he was there, he played basketball. When he got to the main university in the city and talked with the basketball coach there, that coach didn't want him on the team because he only wanted students who would be able to play for four years, not two.

My son was closing out the house that he and a friend were renting in the satellite town. So I went over to help him. His big white dog had been there and was a true digger in the back yard. The dog had brought in and onto the rugs all of the dirt that he could muster from that yard. We had to reclaim the carpet. My son rented a cleaner machine and had to do the job three times. I did the stairs with a scrub brush. We finally had the carpets looking not too bad. One wall was another thing. There was a small hole in the gyproc that someone, not my son, had made. We didn't have time to patch it as it would take time to dry. We were hoping that the landlord was good at fixing things like that or that he would not notice.

For the last year that our son was at that college, a girl had eyed him and invited him to her parents' home for Christmas dinner. He declined to go because he had to be with Sam who was sick. The next year, she invited him again and this time he went because his father had died. That was when she became his steady. Sam had been looked after by my son with the help of the public health nurse. After his father died, my son had to do something about the left over morphine being in the house or he would have had a break-in but I told him to put it all on the porch and when I went west to drive home, I would pick it up and take it to a pharmacy. That solved the problem.

Our son had graduated hls four years of university and wanted to get back to the coast. I went around to several school boards to find out what their hiring policy was and found out that each school district had a different way of hiring. Then a job was advertized in our paper. The newspaper was a small one. Maybe they were desperate. They wanted someone who could coach basketball and also teach computers. My son could do both. I phoned him and gave him the information in the ad and he got the job at that private school in the southern part of the valley.

My son's steady could not concentrate when she was at the university by herself so she quit her course and came to the coast also. She got a job with a finance company but did not like it there. I believe that the boss was hitting on her. They decided to get married.

The wedding was back at the university where the bride's father worked. I offered one of my cousins to do the wedding cake, but the father did not want to pay for very much. I also offered another cousin to do the wedding flowers. These cousins would have worked for almost nothing since I was the one hiring them but the father would not pay for either so they had to buy bulk flowers. It took the couple eight hours to make up the wedding bouquets and flowers for the rows of seats. I had to take my big camera with me to be the photographer, but I got some very good pictures including some with light flashes in them of which I was told were lucky pictures. The marriage itself turned out to be very good, partly because I had had a "man to man" talk with my son, since his father was dead. Since then I sometimes threaten my son as a joke that we would have another heart to heart talk, but he just groans.

The wedding ceremony was over and down the walk came my sister. She had been having a nap at her house and had not woken up in time to get there promptly. She also did not have time to dress up. She had on a long coat, a babushka that she sometimes wore on her head, and was carrying a shopping bag. She looked like a "bag" lady. She often went out dressed like this. There is one in every family! Another family that I knew had a daughter that also was a bit odd. I phoned her one day and asked for her address. She didn't ask why I wanted it but instead said "I'm not giving YOU my address." Well, she missed out. I wanted her address because I had bought her a gift certificate for her birthday. So she never got that birthday present or any other presents after that.

After the wedding, my older son was driving out of the parking lot and his daughter said "Where's Mom?" He didn't have her in the vehicle as she was back still talking with people in the parking lot. He hadn't noticed that she was not in the car and was going to the north without her.

This son of mine, Ralph, lived in the outpost town. He decided to open his own store so he started it in a shopping mall on the hill. This store carried much the same things as the main store downtown, but it was his. Then the shopping mall owner let a very similar store open in the same mall. What bad luck! So the bank got antsy about Ralph's loan and called it in. His father, Bob, would not help him with the bank, so Ralph had to close the store. To get a job, he moved his family back to the city, bought another house, and started a home business as well as working at a job. A few months later his father who was remarried now, came to him, sat on his couch and begged him to come back to the north to be manager of the store. He was sucked in because Ralph and his wife liked the outpost town so they moved again. Everything went fine for a time.

But, one Monday morning Ralph went to work, couldn't get in the store, and realized that the locks had been changed. In other words, he had been relieved of his job without notice. He phoned me to tell me what had happened and I said that I would give it a few minutes to think about it and would call him back. I called him back and said that I believed that his second wife was behind this action and had likely threatened to leave him, like I had, if he didn't do what she wanted. I assumed that she wanted the store or the money for herself and HER son and did not want my son entrenched in that store. So Ralph started a law suit for wrongful dismissal, no notice, slander and a few other charges against his father. The lawsuit dragged on for two years. Then my son gave up because he could see that it was not going anywhere. But that was the end of the relationship with his father who then lost out when he got no further contact with his son, his son's wife, or his two grandchildren. Money isn't everything!

Ralph and his family decided to stay in the northern town even though he was out of a job. His wife still worked so they weren't starving. He started getting a place where he could have a drive through store. It took five years to get a good store up and running well. In this time he sometimes took in newcomers who came to the store looking for work and he helped them get established in Canada and get a license to work.

Then the forest fire ripped through the area. He didn't get his store burned and only one house in the main part of town burned. His house was on the hill, same as the store, and both were saved. Ralph was the only business man who stayed in the town in order to serve the people still there and in the hamlet to the north. The police would come to him every day, take him to his store, and allow him to stay only a certain length of time because of the smoke, then they would collect him and take him home. But he managed to keep the store operating.

After about five years of running this store, he listed it with a company that sold stores and it sold right away. He got quite a lot of money for it because the town was by now in a boom. With this boom, maybe the hospital even got an enema tray and some cloths to go on it.

Ralph's son was living in the hamlet in a condo that he had purchased. The building when he got it had a problem with one corner sinking but only a bit. He had been there a number of years. Then the town decided that the building was sinking too much as it was situated by the river and they were condemning that structure. So Ralph told him that he was flogging a dead horse to keep paying on that suite, so the son had to sell it at a great loss. When he had bought it, I don't know if an appraiser would have spotted the problem or not.

ELEVEN

Since I worked at the hospital in the valley for 23 years, a lot of nurse managers came and went. I was happy looking after patients and not doing paper work even though the nurse manager job would pay more. One day all of the nurses went to lunch and we uleft our nurse manager manning the unit. One of the patients went sour and without looking, the nurse manager got an intravenous that was hung beside the bed and it was ready to go, so she hooked it up as a fast drip. When we came back and saw what she had hung (it had a red label on it), we were surprised because it was exactly the wrong treatment. We stopped the drip and notified the doctor. He said that the patient would likely be all right.

One of our nurses spent quite a bit of time in the bathroom doing her makeup, so this nurse manager put up a notice that said that we could not use the bathroom unless it was our coffee or lunch break. So someone phoned the union and they were there in an hour to put a stop to that idea. It would have been bad if you had come to work with diarrhoea. The nurse who did the makeup got even with the nurse manager because on April Fool's day she put saran wrap over the toilet seat when the nurse manager was going to go into the bathroom.

The next nurse manager was called Suzie. Suzie asked me to her house to have tea. I thought "Isn't that nice. Suzie asked me over for tea." When I got there we had some tea. The tea was only an excuse to get me there. Then, Suzie started in on me saying that I was being irritable at work. She couldn't do this at the hospital, because, if there was a problem, the union would have stepped in. She couldn't complain about my work because I always did a good job and was nice to the patients. Now, why wouldn't I be irritable? I had just signed over my son to his father, was having trouble with the visiting times, my husband had stolen the dog, and I was getting a divorce. That is a lot of problems. Also, I was going home each night and washing walls, sometimes the same walls, to keep my head on straight. Nice to have tea! What a ruse! So I left Suzie's house very dejected. Suzie and her husband weren't so pure. I heard that they had built some duplexes and then rented them as four suites instead of two.

The next nurse manager was the one who didn't like me. She didn't like me because I had a university degree and she didn't have one. I guess that she thought that I could take her job. I could have had that job several times over, but I didn't want a job like that with more paper work and less patient contact. I liked patients. If a patient was conscious, I could get them talking and hear about their life and what they did before they got sick.

So this nurse manager was the one who wanted me out of there. Several times she called me into her office to find out when I was retiring. When she heard that my son was graduating, she was all excited as she thought that I could now retire. I said," He is just graduating from high school and has university to do yet". She was very disappointed. The other nurses told me that when she called me in to her office again to harass me, to demand that a union rep be present.

There was mandatory retirement at age sixty- five at that time. If she had offered me another year, I would have taken it, but she didn't and when I got to another hospital, I worked for another sixteen years for them. I kept working there because they needed a casual nurse who would actually come to work. At the hospital where I was still working, there were several workers in that hospital who were almost seventy years old and still working. But since I was being put out at age sixty-five, they had to retire too. They were given six months to get their affairs in order and then they were done. Not one of them was happy about the situation. They needed money too and I still had my son and his wife at university in Mississippi. I sent them some money each month so i definitely needed money.

So I adjusted a suit that I had at home, got a resume typed by a typing service, got out my briefcase and went out to find another job. I was well educated and well skilled. I went to the local hospital across the river and applied. They said that it was too bad because the day before, they had two similar ICU nurses apply and they had hired them. What they didn't know was that the two nurses were only applying to get the four days orientation money and they could never get them to come to fill a shift. They lost out when they did not hire me.

So I went to the next hospital to the west. Whoever greeted me said, 'Have a seat. I'll get your exam". I was taken aback, but thought, "I am here now, I might as well write the exam". I got a full intensive care exam without any preparation, but the nurse reading my answers was happy with them. When I went back to work where I was still employed, my friends said that they would have walked out.

Two days later I was called to come and sign papers at that new hospital. The papers said that I would be at second year level pay (they actually broke our contract because I was still working at top level salary). I was so happy to have a job that I signed the paper and worked at second level pay for almost ten years. Then the following contract said my wage had to be increased.

At the end of sixteen years working at that hospital, at home I had clunked my head on my car trunk lid and had a bleed in my head. I didn't know what was the matter. I lay on the couch with a headache for a week. Then I went to a walk-in clinic and was told that I had a virus and it would be gone in four days. If I had paid attention to that, I would have died. The next evening, I asked my husband to drive me to the hospital across the river to the emergency department because that hospital had a CAT scanner. The emergency doctor knew in a few minutes what was the matter with me and the CAT scan showed a bleed that was pushing so much on my brain that I was about to die. So much for having a virus! The ambulance screamed me into the city hospital. I had to wait for an operating theatre and I was operated on at two-thirty in the morning.

I was so scared, first, when I saw "Neurological Ward" at the entrance to the ward, and, second, when I was the only one in that ward not screaming all night. In the operating room, the neurosurgeon had doused my head all over with pink antiseptic and I had pink hair for almost two weeks. When visitors stared at me with my pink head, I would say," You pay a lot of money for a hair do like this"

When I was ready for discharge, the neurosurgeon said," Get back to work". He knew how short the intensive care units were for nurses. But, I didn't go back to work and the nurses said,"Can't you even come for four hours?" The area had gotten new computers and the staff was having trouble learning them, so I wasn't going back to have to work on new computers. Now, I was learning how nice retirement was and I was not going to buck it.

TWELVE

Sam was well known in the outpost town. He worked for an electric company in town, but also captained one of the big boats on the river when it went out, which was not too often. Most times the boat was just tied up on the shore, because it was not a boat that carried any freight. Sam let it be known that he had been to band school, was capable of being a band master, and was anyone interested in being in a band. There were a lot of volunteers for the band, including Bob, my two children, and myself. Bob and I signed up and signed up the children. Sam was getting our instruments from a company that he knew in the east. Everyone who was to be in the band picked or was allotted an instrument to buy and to learn to play. Bob picked a snare drum. I picked an alto saxophone like my cousin played, our son was allotted a coronet, and our daughter a clarinet.

When the instruments arrived, we went to a meeting and were shown each instrument in turn and told some of the things not to do with an instrument such as push a mouthpiece into the instrument so that it wouldn't come out. We were to just set the mouthpiece into the instrument and give it a little twist. The people with the reed instruments were shown how to look after their reeds and how to put one in. I realized right away that I already had a favorite reed for my saxophone.

We were all sent home to blow on our instruments, except there wasn't a point in blowing on the snare drum. By the end of a few days, we should have a firm enough "lip" to start to play. We were not to puff out our cheeks when blowing. Bob practiced with his drumsticks on the kitchen table. By the following week we were ready.

Mostly we produced squawks but gradually as the weeks rolled along, we got some music to come out. By then we could all read the music not too badly. The worst days were over. Then we learned to march. Sam marched in front of us and did some signalling with his silver baton that had a yellow cord in a pattern. He was the one who wrapped the pattern around it. He knew all the signals for us to start to play. Bob with his snare drum was one of the drummers who led us into a piece. He was very proud. Du-du, du-du, brrrer. I can still hear the drum sound for us to start playing. We marched with pride and in line down the main street.

The town with the help of many ironworkers was building a bridge across the large river so a road could be made to the next northern town. Finally the bridge was ready and who were the first people to go across the bridge? It was the band members playing and marching remarkably well. We didn't have uniforms, but we wore white cotton tops and black bottoms. The white really made us stand out and the sound, we thought, was terrific. The whole ceremony was very impressive and finished off with us playing "God Save the Queen". Once again, the mayor was very proud for the town which now had a new bridge and an accomplished band.

Sam was a good band master and since I was near the front of the band with my saxophone and Bob was at the back with his drum, I saw more of Sam than of Bob who still worked eighty hours a week and did not take his weekly half day off. I was without a husband most of my time and had to find my own things to do.

When I had finally decided to leave the hamlet, Sam was the one who helped me and got me the accommodation with his friends near the coast. I didn't know it at the time, but Sam was already thinking that if I could leave, he might be able to leave also, since his marriage had been a shambles for a long time. So the band, if he left, would be without the three of my family in it and without a band master. Perhaps someone else in the band would be able to take over.

The next band that Sam started was when we were in a northern town also. The next town east to where we lived, had asked him to get a band going. So he did. By that time, I had my little girl. When I had taken her home from the hospital, she was fed, dry, and still kept screaming. I didn't know what she wanted. Finally I figured out that she wanted to be bundled with the blankets tight around her like she had been in the hospital. So I wrapped her up and she was happy. We were building another house and had it partly done but the hole for the fireplace and brick chimney in the living room was still open. The brick layer man had not come yet. So I phoned him and told him that it was getting colder outside and my little baby was sometimes cold. He came the next day so we had the space closed and could have a fire.

My husband and I were both working in the back bedrooms and the German Shepherd that we had was by the fireplace. A cinder jumped out of the fire and onto the floor. That dog came to us in the back rooms and barked and barked until we went to see what the matter was. We found a cinder on the wooden floor. The smart dog made his keep that day. Luckily there was not a hole in the floor yet.

Sam was organizing the band and one day he came home and said "I have sold your saxophone to another player. I want you to play a brass instrument to strengthen the band. You can play the Conn trombone that we have". A Conn trombone is a good one. So I had only a few days to learn the trombone. I found out that I liked the trombone and liked the sound that it made. It was fun to slide the slide. So when I played, I put some cotton in my little girl's ears to cut the sound and crooked her in my left arm. That left my right arm free to work the slide. She got to really like the music especially the marches. When we played a march, she was very happy.

Coming home on the highway, two things happened. First, Sam was driving and I noticed a reddish glow out the back window. When I turned around to look, I could see an oval, reddish object hovering over the highway in the distance. I told Sam to step on it as I assumed that it looked like and likely was a flying saucer that I had seen in pictures in magazines. We didn't waste time getting away from it.

The second thing that I saw on another night, was an object over in a field. The object looked about seven feet tall and was walking. Since it was almost all dark outside, it was hard to identify it properly, but I assumed that it was a sasquatch as they had been seen in that area a few weeks before. Again, we did not stop to investigate.

Another strange thing happened when I was back at home. I always baked my bread. I had made two loaves and had them on the breadboard on the counter. After they are cooked, I turn them out there to cool and air, turning them over periodically to dry all of the sides. There was time before supper, so I went to the store to get a few groceries. When I came home and entered the house, I could not believe my eyes. One of the fresh loaves of bread was sitting in the middle of my kitchen floor, about six feet from where I had left the two loaves on the breadboard. Since I don't have a dog, a cat, or rodents and have an alarm system on my house, no one had been there. The only thing that I could think of was that a ghost had moved it. After that, someone told me that the ghost was trying to tell me something, but I don't imagine what that would be.

When we had the weekly band practices in that town near to where we lived, we had a good workout. We would play through an entire small book of Sousa marches and then play most of our other music. I played second trombone. The first trombone player was called Jose and he, like me could really play. Jose had just separated from his wife so he was happy to have a night out with his music friends. Pretty soon, Jose started to date a lady in the town who had lost her husband to sickness more than ten years ago. In all of that time, she kept his memory pure and never went dating with anyone. She was reluctant to go out with Jose, but soon they were thick and he moved in with her. She was happy. The couple put the cart before the horse and went on a trip together to Mexico, almost like a honeymoon. Lucy had a credit card and was paying for the trip. By this time, she was infatuated with Jose so she let him buy things and charge them to her charge card. Jose bought mostly nice shirts, quite a few. They were also staying in a four star hotel and the meals were expensive.

When they got home, while Lucy was at work, Jose left with his new clothes, his trombone, and his truck. Lucy was also left but with an eight thousand dollar charge card bill to pay. She was not so upset with the amount of the purchases as she was with the fact that she had lived with a man after being true to the memory of her dead husband for so long.

In that band in the town, we had a man with tunnel vision. He still worked in the town office, but with a lot of difficulty. He could play the oboe. To learn to play the music, he would take it home and memorize all of the music note by note. When we marched, he went behind a girl with a blond head and followed her head so that he was marching in the proper way. He coped really well. The girl with the blond head was one of four musical children of a European man who also was playing in the band and he played a bass horn, like a sousaphone. So there were five from that family in the band. At home to practice, they played hymns which suited the family fine.

By this time the band had purchased second hand uniforms that were brown with orange trim. A new road was going through to lead farther to the north, and the band was asked to play for the opening of this road, so we wore the uniforms. We didn't pay to be in the band, we only donated our time, but when we played at a place, the officials often donated us some money. That is how we paid for the uniforms and could buy some music when we needed it. Buying the music meant that we had to have music for each instrument to play, sometimes two or more copies.

The premier of the province was at the opening to give a speech. When the occasion was over, some of us got to ride in the limo with him. He was very friendly in talking with us and said that he enjoyed our playing.

Sam and I had built an A-frame house in the town where we lived. One day a little black dog came to our door. He was scraggy and hungry. I fed him, cleaned him up, made some notices, and went into the town to put up the notices. I also asked around if someone was missing a dog. My little girl could not say "Puppy" so he became "Popey". We had that dog for quite a while and no one claimed him. Then he went missing. So I went out in the car to look for him. I found him in a trailer park, running in a pack of other dogs, all bigger than he was. I had looked after this dog for over two months so I went to the police and told them about him, that I had tried to find an owner, and where I had found him was running loose with the dog pack. The police told me that by now he was my dog and to take him back home. They said that they did not like dogs running in a pack because they often caused trouble. We had that dog for many years and he always lay beside my daughter's playpen to guard her.

When the work gave out for Sam, we moved to a central province town and then the following move was to a city in the lower mainland. There was already a band in the new city and Sam was not the bandmaster. The band already had a band master so Sam sat in the front row and played his clarinet. I sat in the trombone section and got the second trombone music. The first trombone player was a young lad who soon went away to agricultural school. The band master rounded up an even younger boy and put him in the first trombone chair. The bandmaster was also giving this boy private lessons. But the boy knew only a little about music and timing so I had to help him a lot. There came along a trombone solo and the bandmaster gave the solo to this not very musical boy. I had played in that band quite a long time so to not get the solo made me very upset, I'd say angry.

At the end of the band practice, I went to the back of the room where there were extra band instruments. There was a single French horn on the shelf that seemed to be in good shape. So I took it home, bought a book on how to play the French horn and within three days, I could play it. For the next band practice, I took only the French horn, sat in the horn section, and asked the other players for the third horn music. The bandmaster looked at me in a horn chair and not in a trombone chair and almost dropped his teeth to his boots. He had lost his good trombone player. Inside, I was laughing. I liked that horn, so in a few weeks, I ordered and bought myself an Olds double French horn and returned the single horn to the back of the band room. We continued playing in that band for a few months, then we went to play with the band in a town a little farther away as we thought it had a better band. They were happy to have us.

My marriage was getting quite rocky at this point. Beside me at band practice sat a church minister who played third trumpet. He and I got quite friendly. Sam was furious. The minister knew that I was unsettled due to my marriage problems and started taking me out in his car after band practice. He was only counselling me, but the effect on Sam was not good. I was feeling better with the counselling in spite of Sam being so angry. It wasn't long afterwards that Sam and I split up.

Now, for entertainment I joined a singles club. I tried one out in the next town, but they were not a very friendly bunch, but the one that I joined was like a big family. We had parties, picnics, and sometimes dancing. There was a man who went and was called Jim. Jim liked me and would work all day in a sawmill and then in the evening would come over the bridge to see me. He was working in the mill to save enough money to keep buying rentals until he had enough rent money coming in to live off of it. He ended up with twenty-two rentals, a few of them owned with a partner called Ned.

At that time there was quite a bit of crime in the city where I lived. One night two girls were out walking and they were attacked by a mugger. One was able to run like crazy, but the other one was stabbed with a knife and died on the spot. The attacker got away and no one knew who he was. So for weeks, in the evenings, the city was deserted. No joggers were out, no dog walkers were out, no one on a bicycle was out, no one walking and only a scattering of cars on the streets. Everyone was afraid.

The police were not getting anywhere with finding the murderer. Then they got a tip. As it happened, the tip came from the man's mother. She actually turned him in. A few nights before the girls had been attacked, this man had had a bar-be-que at his house which was only two doors away from the house where the dead girl had lived. It is hard to believe, but the two girls were at his bar-be-que. So he was caught, arrested and the people in the city could again stroll about in the evenings.

The next problem was right near my house. I was sitting by the front window and heard a noise. So I looked out and saw a young man running from my back yard, to across the street, and he was naked. He was shaking some keys in one hand and yelling at two people outside the house there. That house was the original house from the apple orchard on which the subdivision was built. I assumed that the people were his parents. What he was yelling was" You can't go in the house. It is my house now and I own it". The two people looked quite frightened so I phoned to the police to tell them what was going on. When the police came, the parents told them that this naked young man was their son and that they were sure that he had stopped taking his medication and that that was what was the matter with him. They also said that he was a schizophrenic, according to the psychiatrist. The policemen said that they would take the boy to the hospital where he would get some medication. Then they wrapped a blanket around him. After they left with the boy, the parents had the house keys back and got into their house. The neighbourhood was quite now.

A few weeks later, I met the mother outside and I asked her how her son was doing. She told me that when he got back on his pills, he was fine, and that he now had a job and a girl friend. He was still living at home, but all was peaceful. She said that normally her son was a decent lad but always needed his medication.

THIRTEEN

When I was living in the province's central town, my sister phoned me one night at ten p.m. It would be eleven p.m. in the next province where she lived. My mother, I knew, was in the hospital for a time and my sister was frantic. She almost screamed into the phone "They're going to discharge mother". I said,"You mean at ten o'clock at night?" She replied "No, but they are going to put her out." "Well, I said, I will phone the hospital in the morning".

The next morning, I phoned to the hospital and told them that I could not come there until the end of the week, but then I would take her out. When I got to the hospital and talked with the doctor, he asked if I wanted a list of her medications. I said no, that I could remember them.

From the hospital, Sam and I took my mother to her house in the same city, and because she was coming home with me to the next province, my sister and I had to sort out a number of items that we had previously stored in a cedar lined room in her basement. My sister was very greedy, as usual, and wanted almost everything. I let her take most of the things as I had enough of my own items at home.

Before we left the city, my mother wanted to sell a good chesterfield and chair for three hundred dollars, but no one bought it. So I said that we had better load it onto the trailer that we had rented and take it. What else could we do with it? A few weeks later my sister accused me of stealing the set and until the day that my sister died, she never let up about it. I hadn't needed that furniture and eventually sold my own chesterfield and chair to keep the good set which I later had recovered.

My mother was happy at my house and said that it was now her home. Every day she went out for a short walk down the street, weak as she was. When the old man across the street would see her go out, he would go out and walk with her. Sometimes he had to help her home.

This man had often been a patient of mine in the hospital and his doctor arranged with me that if he had some heart pain, the family that he lived with would call me over and I would give him a little bit of morphine. They had the morphine, not me. The man and family that he lived with had come to the town together, had built a big house, and had items like four snow mobiles, four dune buggies and seemed to have lots of money. The lady especially loved this old man as did the whole family. I knew that they had been in Chicago, so one day I asked him about it. He got a twinkle in his eyes and said "What do you know about Chicago?" About the time that I figured that they had been there was the time that the big mob boss was running Chicago. I got thinking about the closeness of the old man and the lady. What I could think of was that the mob boss had a lot of lady friends and that one of them had had a baby, his baby. His girl friends would no doubt be beautiful and my neighbour lady was also beautiful. l figured out that the old man, young then, who lived with the family might have been a patsy, or somebody working for the crime boss and he would not have been good enough to work in the crime scene, but he would be good enough to be the babysitter for this baby. The crime boss would not want this baby around his mob as she got older. The big boss would need a man to babysit because he did not keep women in his employ. He also realized that this man that I knew was fond of the baby so he chose him.

I also thought that the old man had saved his money, stolen it, or more likely, had been given a big payout to disappear somewhere even over the border to Canada and to take the baby with him. Where they were living now was a long way from Chicago. I also thought that when the mob boss found out that the man and the baby had disappeared, he would be happy, because he was too busy doing drive by shootings, selling illegal whiskey, and organizing his crew to extol money from merchants and he didn't want to be concerned about anything else, especially a baby.

So when the old man would not talk to me about Chicago and was smirking about it, I knew that he would never guess that I could figure it out as well as I did. No one would be as close to a person as he was to the lady unless he had raised her and that he had taken her away from the crime scene. Perhaps his name was even on the birth certificate even though he was not the father because the mob boss would not want his name to be on the birth certificate. So when the heart pain came, I went over and gave him his shot for relief and said no more.

When I had brought my mother to live with me, I did not realize that she was as sick as she was. Within three weeks I had to put her in the hospital. The nurses would get her into the chair each day and she would put her embroidery in her lap to pretend that she was working on it. Then she suddenly died. A few weeks later when I was in the bathroom at night, I saw her image walk in front of the door and down the hall. She had come home where she had been happy, but she was already dead when i visualized her.

Across the lane at the back of our house lived a doctor. He and his wife had two almost grown children. The daughter became a drug addict. That fact was fairly well known in the city where we lived. In order to keep the daughter from stealing or doing other bad things in order to buy drugs, the doctor wrote prescriptions for her to get the drugs. He knew that he stood a chance of losing his medical license by doing this but what was he going to do? Then one night he was on call for the hospital and the call that came for him, was a motorcycle accident. When he got to the accident a policeman told him to move out of the way, not realizing that he was the doctor. The doctor said "This is my son". The boy was taken to the hospital but died in the night. Now he only had the drug addict daughter left and his wife, who was so shaken that she became a recluse.

FOURTEEN

My daughter, Betty, lived in the big city in the next province from where I lived. She wanted to have a business for herself so she bought a small distributorship for kitchen machines. She bought it from a friend who couldn't seem to make a living with it. Betty's husband built her some shelves in their basement. She was very personable so the business prospered. It was doing so well, that they moved it to a rented space in a small shopping mall in the downtown area. In this store they built in the back room a complete kitchen with an overhead mirror where Betty could teach classes using the machines that she sold. She trained her staff to help her with the classes. Trent stayed in the front of the store and after each class, the participants could purchase what they needed to do their cooking at home. Trent also built Betty a trailer so she could go out to the rural areas to do trade shows. The shows produced a lot of business. Next, a friend that she knew and who was hostess on a morning TV show would have her do demonstrations on the TV so the business started to boom. All of the farm people and others watched my daughter do her demonstrations on the T.V. show. She became well known and that was good for business.

Now they needed more space so they moved the store to a larger space in another mall. Here they had to again build a new kitchen in the back of the store because the classes had expanded to include things like chocolate making.

Because they were very busy, they wanted to build a better and bigger house so they bought a lot on a man made lake in the south east of the city. They did not have time to drive to a cottage at a far away lake so this suited them. I suggested that the builders double the floor joists under the living room where there was an inside wall so I could give her my piano. However, Trent thought it too expensive to move the piano there so she didn't get it.

The house that they built had two garages, a basement with bathroom between two bedrooms, a rec room with a bar, and some exercise equipment. The main floor had a large dining room, a kitchen with a large centre island, an office, a bathroom, a pantry, a laundry room, and a large living room with an alcove off of it for every day eating. When we sat in this eating area, we could look out over the lake. On the lake they had a dock and two paddle boats tied to it. The small back yard that stopped at the lake had enough space for a few raised beds for gardens.

When I travelled to the city to see my son who was at university there, I sometimes had supper at my daughter's house but never stayed the night. When I contacted Betty that I was coming to the city, she asked me to supper when I got there. She said that she was having a Pastor from the next town for supper also that night. When I got there, I was introduced to the Pastor and we sat down to eat. We were almost through the meal when the Pastor asked me where I was staying. He knew that I wasn't staying with Betty because I had come in the front door.

I said" Well, it's cheaper to stay in a campground than in a hotel so I'm staying in the campground on the west side of the city and I'm sleeping in my tent". The Pastor replied,"There is this big house and you are staying in a tent?" He looked very surprised and started to laugh. I said" I have an arctic sleeping bag and I am quite warm". He kept laughing and laughing. Pretty soon others at the table started laughing and I was laughing too. The Pastor kept on with the joke and three times he turned to me and said "Are you all right?" I replied that I was O.K. The laughing didn't stop. He was making a huge amount of fun of the fact of the big house and I was sleeping in a tent. It really was funny. Finally the dinner was over and I left to go back to my campground.

After I had left, I believe that the Pastor asked my daughter how the tent situation had happened. My daughter just said that her mother was very independent. So, I think that the Pastor told her that what was happening was not right. So everything changed and I was afterwards welcome in her house. She also became very nice to me and as time went on we became close.

A few months later when I went back to the city, I was able to stay in Betty's basement room and was made welcome in her and Trent's home. When I would wake up in the morning, I could look through the window and see their dock, the paddle boats, and the lake. There were big houses all around the lake and the beach for the swimming was straight across from where I was.

When I had come in to the cul-de-sac where Betty's house was, I had noticed across the street and a few houses down, a truck that said "Rug Cleaning" on it and a small sign on it that said "organic cleaning". A man got out of the truck and I remembered his looks. He was over six feet tall, well built, and had bright red hair that was tied in a pony-tail. He couldn't be missed as he was so distinguished looking.

The next morning when I woke up, I looked around the blind on the window to see the lake. The colors on the lake in the early morning were always different according to the sun. But this morning I noticed that one of Trent's paddle boats was missing. It was out on the lake and the cleaning man with the big build and the red pony-tail was in the boat paddling it to the middle of the lake. Beside him was a roll that looked like it was a rolled up rug. Now I knew what the "organic cleaning" was. The cleaner dipped your rug in the lake. However, I was glad that it was not my rug because the red haired man put the rug in the water but did not pull it out. He let go of the rug, gave it a push and it went down to Davy Jones's Locker. From the speed that the roll sank, I suspected that there was something in it like a body and that this was a murder. Mr. Pony-tail paddled the boat back to our dock but without the roll with him. So much for the organic cleaning!

I had to wait until Trent got up to tell him what I had seen. He phoned the police. So a police car came to the house and Trent told them what I had seen and I confirmed it. The policemen went back to their patrol car and one of them opened the trunk and took out a fishing rod. Then they went down to the dock which by now had the two paddle boats tied up to it. Instead of looking at both boats to see which one had been recently used, they just got into one. It was too bad that the one that they got into was the one that Mr. Red Pony-tail had used. There went away any fingerprints that could be taken from that boat.

The policemen both paddled the little boat out to where I had pointed out that the heavy rug had been let go. Their next action was very funny. They were trying to latch on to the rug roll and pull it up with their fishing line. By this time most of the people who lived around the lake had come out to see what was happening and there was also a small crowd watching from the beach. The policemen realized that the fishing rod was not going to do the job so they paddled the boat back to the dock. One of them got a phone out of his breast pocket and made a call.

Soon more police cruisers arrived and the men brought down to the lake some diving equipment. So they had two men and diving equipment to go out for the rug roll. One of the policemen had to hold the oxygen tank on his lap as well as help to paddle the boat. The one diver, with effort, got into his diving suit and down he went. He had to make two tries but he was able to bring up the roll on the second dive. He had been a diver in the navy in the Second World War so was quite skillful in diving.

The next door neighbour had watched what was going on and realized that the policemen had too much of a load to bring to shore, so he paddled out in his canoe to help them. He took the roll and struggled to get it into the canoe. He almost got it in when the canoe tipped over and again down the rug went. More organic cleaning! The diver saw what was happening and quickly went down to bring it up. This time the three men got the canoe upright and positioned the rug more carefully in it. The oxygen tank and everything else was put into the canoe also and all came to the shore. When the rug roll was opened, there truly was a dead body inside and there was a bullet hole in the middle of the forehead of the unfortunate man. This was not a suicide for sure! I was a light sleeper but since I was sleeping in a basement room at the time, I had not heard a gunshot sound. Maybe he had been shot elsewhere.

Soon a photographer showed up and the morgue wagon also. Yellow tape was being put around our dock, around the canoe, and around the van in front of red ponytail's house. When all of the work and investigation seemed to be done, Mr. Ponytail was put in handcuffs and was taken off to the pokey. Since the big excitement was over, everyone went back into their houses. We thanked the next door neighbour for using his canoe to help out. Trent and I couldn't do any more outings on the lake since the paddle boats were closed in with yellow police tape. When I said goodbye to Betty and Trent to drive home, I had lots to think about because what we had seen and experienced was the real thing and better than any murder novel that I liked to read.

By this time when I was driving home, the evening was closing in but I decided to make some more miles before I pulled in for the night. When I was almost to the mountains, the weather changed to snow but I kept going.

I got a little farther down the road and something in my head said "Go back. There is something on the road". I kept going. Again the same thing came into my head with the same message "Go back". I thought that I might be dreaming, but I was wide awake. That's why I was still driving. The third time that I heard the voice telling me to go back, I paid attention and decided that somehow I was being warned. So I turned around and went back to the closest town. The snow was not coming down too fast so the driving was still good. I pulled in to a motel and stayed the night. Going down the road in the morning, I didn't see anything strange or anything on the road, but at least I was safe.

FIFTEEN

Up the road and around the corner to the south of James's farm, lived Ned and Jodie. They were friends and became partners with James. When they all bought one of their rental properties with eleven rentals on it and east of the city, James brought the papers for the purchase home for me to read. When I read them I said "This is not right. These papers are made out for three people. It says the property is for Ned Ryan, Jodie Ryan, and James Cowie. That means that you will be one third owner, but you are paying for half of the property. The papers have to be redone so that they read Ned Ryan with Jodie Ryan together and James Cowie." So the papers went back to the lawyer and were made out again. James would have lost big time if the original papers had been used. Ned Ryan and Jodie Ryan were one entity buying the property together as man and wife then James was buying his half and that is how the redone papers read. James was saved!

Ned and Jodie had a small hobby farm. The house was up on the hill as well as a makeshift barn close to it. They kept sheep that in the daytime grazed on the hill in front of the house. In that field were also two donkeys. Both donkeys had coats to wear outside of the barn. One had a blue coat and one had a red coat. They were very protective of their coats as if they were a status symbol. If you tried to but the wrong coat on one of the donkeys, it would stamp it's front feet and bray with a snorting noise. The donkeys didn't work or do anything except eat but they did keep the coyotes away from the sheep. The sheep at least produced wool.

Next door on a hobby farm, the neighbour had four donkeys. This farmer claimed that his donkeys could count to four. He had built two carts for the donkeys to pull. One cart was smaller and it took two donkeys to pull it. The other cart which was larger had to be pulled by the four donkeys.

This farmer obtained and was paid for gigs such as fairs, galas, and home parties. Since he got paid, the rides for the children were free. The donkey rides were popular so he got to go to a lot of festivities thus the animals earned their keep.

The night before an outing, the farmer would tell the donkeys that two of them would go out the following day and he would say the names of the two or he would tell them that four of them would work the next day. The donkeys never made a mistake. The following morning the correct donkeys would be waiting at the gate to get hooked up to a cart.

In the farmer's will he had put that when he died, the donkeys were to be put down because he didn't trust anyone, even his wife, to be kind to his donkeys.

A little farther down the road, a pipe came out of the mountain on the east side of the road and the water that flowed out of the pipe was very pure. Many people including all the neighbours got their drinking water from the flow from that pipe. There was also a pipe like that on the east side of the city but the town shut it down and removed it because the officials said it was not safe. That was not really true. People had been using that water for years and even one man came with his truck and filled large bottles with the water and sold them. Then, the town officials tried to shut down the pipe with the water flowing on the west side of the city, near to the property where the donkeys lived, but the local people guarded that pipe day and night and finally the removers gave up. No one knew from where the water came but it was some place inside the mountain that a smart person had figured out that there was water there and it could be tapped into for the benefit of the locals. So that pipe and water was saved.

Ned Ryan who lived close by noticed that there was a black car parked on the road opposite his small farm. The car was there every night. So Ned called the police to come and investigate why that car was there. A squad car came and two policemen checked it out, then they got back to Ned to explain to him that it was the revenue service of the government that was trying to find out why their neighbour claimed only a very small amount of income year after year. The amount of the income was not enough on which he could live. So the car stayed every night and observed that the hobby farmer left his property each night with his truck which seemed to be weighted down well on the road as though it had a load on. A few hours later the truck came back and this time it was bouncing along on the dirt road as though it was very empty and light. So they knew that the farmer had delivered something before he came home.

Still wanting to know more, the revenue people got a search warrant to investigate further. When they got to the property with the warrant, the farmer had to let them search everything.. What they found was that this man had stocks of bottled whiskey in his basement, all new. They were also shocked to find that he had a still in a back shed and that he was making moonshine, popular with people who had a low income and couldn't afford the store bought bottles of liquor. Near the apparatus were empty bottles that looked clean and shiny, waiting to get the homemade liquid poured into them. They assumed that when the truck went out each night it was full of bottles of moonshine. So the poor farmer owed huge amounts for back taxes on his delivery proceeds but was also in deep with the police for doing an illegal business. On his income tax reporting he had not shown any amounts of income from this side line business which was really a full time occupation. The revenue men were happy because their stake out and warrant had paid off. They only thought of themselves and didn't care that the hobby farm man was ruined. We never saw the farmer again and in a few months the property was up for sale, moonshine still and all. His patrons in the city must have been distraught that their whiskey supply was gone. The black car that had done the stake out was never seen again.

SIXTEEN

When Ned, James's partner, was driving out to the eastern rental properties, a vehicle coming towards him on the road had a small trailer on the back of the truck. This trailer got loose and came towards Ned, smashing into his truck. The bump wasn't too bad but Ned complained and complained about his neck being sore as he had been thrown into the windshield. The case about his neck went to the court and he kept on about his neck. The x-rays showed that he had some arthritis in his neck and it was of a long standing duration. However, he kept complaining about his neck so finally he got a fairly large payout. The arthritis remained but the money that he got made him laugh all his way to the bank.

Ned and Jodie had two almost grown boys, but they had always wanted a girl. So they applied to the child welfare services for a child, that, if satisfactory, would be adopted by them. They were approved for an orphan. Because it was a hobby farm, the system sent them a boy. The lad was about nine years old but hardly spoke. But what he was good at was eating. Perhaps he was related to the donkeys that they had because all that they did was eat and eat.

So Jodie asked me to come over to see what I thought of this boy. Because he was reluctant to speak at all. I was not impressed with him. So they sent him back saying that they had asked for a girl.

When a lovely girl came in a taxi, she was eight years old. She was a beautiful child and had attractive and expensive clothes. She also had a purse with her and she clutched onto it tightly. Her mother and father had put her into child care because they said that they could not handle her. Did they think that Ned and Jodie could do better? So she was there and they moved her into her bedroom. Then for two nights they realized that this child did not sleep. She napped a bit in the daytime, but at night, it was hopeless. Since they had stayed awake with her for two nights, for the third night and thereafter they hired a lady to come and look after this girl at night so that they could sleep. The child rustled around the house all night. One evening the couple brought her to my house to visit. The girl wanted desperately to stay at my house overnight, no doubt to rifle my house the same as she had done at the hobby farm, but they did not allow her to stay with me, thank goodness, and they took her back to their farm.

Soon Jodie noticed that the girl's purse seemed to be getting fatter and fatter so with difficulty they got the purse from her and looked into it. The girl had a tantrum. What they found in the purse was three rings, two necklaces, and a lot of dollars that the couple had been saving in a jar that was like an extra bank. Well, that was the limit! What she was doing, especially at night, was searching the house for whatever she could get into her purse. The parents of the girl had told the child welfare that their girl could not get along at school either. No wonder, because she helped herself to anything that she fancied.

So Jodie and Ned put the girl back into a taxi since that is how she had come to them and sent her back to social services. That was the end of trying to get a readymade child.

But luck was with them. Their second son had conceived a child with his girl friend and when it was born, it was a girl. The father had joint custody of the baby so every other weekend he brought the child home with him and Jodie got to tend to it. As the child grew, Jodie and Ned taught the girl all that they could. Even as a child she became quite expert with a computer. When I got my computer and was having trouble learning it, James, my husband, said that I needed Rose, then five, to help me.

When Rose was getting a bit older, she asked if her half brother, who was a year older, could come with her on the alternate weekend visits. She wanted him to come because the food that they got at their mother's home was a bit scant and at Jodie's house the food was good with lots of it. The influence that the children got at Ned's and Jodie's home was very helpful in making good people of those children. Jodie had her girl that she had wanted but also got a boy, who was also a prize for them.

When Ned and Jodie's older son had a fiancé called Heidi and they were going to get married, the family rented the bigger community hall in the area. They planned a sit down dinner followed by a dance with a live band. All was arranged but there was one problem.

Not one of them in the family could dance and the bride and groom had to do the first dance which would be a wedding waltz. So Jodie asked me if I could teach them to dance. It was two months to the wedding.

As a young child, I had been taken to the farm dances by my uncle and family when we visited them. My cousin played his saxophone at the dances and his sister played keyboard. There were also some guitar players. So I got to watch all the dances, listen to the music and take it all in. When I got sleepy, I would curl up on a bench along the wall and go to sleep. At the end of the dance the family would scoop me up and carry me to the car to go home. I was still asleep but the music and dancing were firmly imbedded in my head.

I told Ned and Jodie that if I was going to teach them to dance, we would have to have dancing lessons 101. We arranged for twice a week. James was not a problem since he could dance and he was my partner. So I taught them first the box waltz because that was the dance with which the bride and groom would open the dancing. I told them that if they did not do it nicely they would hear me from across the room calling" Step, two, three, step, two, three".

Besides the box waltz, I taught them to fox-trot, twist (a new dance), one step, jive, polka, and schottische. They had trouble learning to jive until I told them to pretend that they were a rag doll with no control of their limbs. That worked.

We practiced in their living room at the farm by removing the coffee table and rolling back the rugs. The couple was embarrassed that no one in the family could dance, so when we saw a car starting to come up their long driveway to visit, we put the rugs and the coffee table back in place and sat quietly like angels. This sometimes happened more than once in an evening. We couldn't wait for each group to leave since two months was not long to learn to dance. But they mastered the skill. I told Ned that he and his wife were to get up for each dance to at least start it so that the guests would get onto the dance floor. Some of the women danced together. As I moved along throughout the evening, I heard lots of comments that the people did not know that the host family members could dance. Believe it or not the family did a remarkable job and the box waltz done by the bride and groom was beautiful. So the dance lessons 101 were a success. Move over dance teachers!

SEVENTEEN

When I first met James Cowie, it was at a single's club party. He had had two drinks and was out of this world. The next time that I met him he was stone sober and he asked if he could take me home. He came to my house in his yellow truck and came inside for coffee. Then he started coming to my house to visit every evening after he worked at the mill. James always had coffee when he came because he liked coffee. At the mill, he was a packer of cedar shakes. After several weeks on a Sunday, he said that he wanted to show me something. So we went for a drive and finally ended up at what he said was the farm house that he had built. That is where he lived. The house was on two adjacent pieces of property that were almost five acres each. In the valley where we lived, that was a lot of property and it was worth a lot of money. He had kept the secret of where he lived until he had courted me for quite a long time. Below his property on the next piece of land was his mother's property and below that and a little down the hill was his sister's property.

When James had built his house, he had bought a sling of lumber from the mill to do it so he had lots of lumber. When he was part way along with the building, his cow ate the house plans. He was now on his own to do the house. I was amused when I saw how he had done some of the corners inside the closets. Instead of putting in two boards that were two by four, he put in four. That house was going to be really sturdy.

After several months of James still coming every night to my house to see me, he asked me to come and take a try at living with him. He said that in six months we would get married. He really did say that! So I put my things into storage, sold my house, and moved to the farm. If he had not said that we would get married, I would not have moved there.

James had two children. John was fifteen and Joan was fourteen. The boy was somewhat head strong and would sneak out every evening and come home late and staggering drunk. He wouldn't take his hat off at the table which annoyed as I considered that bad manners, and he was generally disruptive. Later when he was older, he was diagnosed as being schizophrenic. I couldn't do much with him but he did love my biscuits.

When Joan was doing her school work, I noticed that she did not know what some of the words like "senate" meant. She had been in the small country school so that accounted for her lack of some knowledge. Next, I started helping her and she quickly picked up on everything so that she graduated her last grade of high school.

Joan had never had a job. She tried a few things like chicken catching but she only worked one night because the chickens pecked at her. Next, she tried the burger outlet. That didn't last very long. Then James got her to take a course in hairdressing where she did very well.

However, she never took the apprenticing that followed the course, so she couldn't get a job. I persuaded James to give her at the college a short course in cashier training, but she never went after a job for that. As long as James gave her money she was content. One day when she asked for money, I said to James "Do you realize that you have given her money three times already today?" He had forgotten that.

James taught his son how to pack the shakes into a bundle for the mill. The boy learned quickly and could make a good bundle very fast. That was all that it took to get a job. But he didn't stick with it.

When I got moved in to the farm house, I was surprised at how someone batching with two almost grown children living there could not keep the house better. I found under the sink, five pounds of coffee and six bags of potatoes that were sprouting big time. Also, in the basement his children were growing marijuana plants in one corner. For a while, James had taken in his daughter's friend who did not get along with her parents. But after some weeks he realized that it was not good to have a young girl not related to him living in his house since he was divorced. So he told her that she had to find another place to live. She ended up going to the arctic where we learned that she had married a local man there and was having numerous children.

After I cleaned up the kitchen and got the stove fixed, I decided to do some wall painting. The living room had shag wall to wall carpet in it. The carpet was somewhat out of style, but it was in good shape and the walls didn't need painting. What I worked on was the two small bedrooms.

The daughter's room was in not too bad condition for painting and was easy to paint. But the son's room had to have a lot of work. John, James's son had a cough, possibly from chain smoking, and when he coughed at night, he hacked onto the walls. It was disgusting. So before I could paint, I had to scrape the walls to remove the dried mess and this took a long time and a lot of scraping. At last I could do the painting and the room was looking very nice. In order to keep the son from sneaking out at night, James nailed the window shut but that didn't stop him. He managed to get out some way so he and a friend could go drinking. He would never remember in the morning what the two of them had done the night before and would be on the phone to his friend, asking what they had done.

When six months was up, I reminded James that he had told me before I moved to his hobby farm that we would get married if all went well for that six month period. However, he said that he had never said that. What is the matter with people who lie all the time? First, Bob had told me that we would live for one year in the northern hamlet and then return to the city to live. That was the first lie. Second, James said that he had never said that we would likely get married in six months. That was his lie. Both of these men told the lies to me to get what they wanted. After several years, I was glad that James and I had not become married because then I would be mother- in- law to John, the son, who was a hopeless person who wasn't my type at all. We would have clashed all the time.

James was at work on the evening shift. The payoff came when I was on my day off from work. I had waited all day to watch the movie at eight p.m. When the movie came on and I turned to the channel, John switched the channel to what he wanted. I turned the channel back to the movie. Three times John turned the T.V. to his show. At the third time, he actually raised his arm to hit me. That was the limit!

At the same time the renters that were in the house that I had purchased in the city, moved out. They said that they were moving out because the drapery cord was broken. Really? I told them that I had a tool to fix that and that I was good at doing so. But they had already vacated. The timing was perfect as I decided that I would move from the farm where John had almost hit me and live in my own house in town. After that episode with John, when he came to my house to see his father I would never let him in. He had to wait on the porch. And he never ever got invited for dinner where there might be biscuits that he loved.

As I was getting ready to move, I told James to make up his mind. Was he coming to town with me or wasn't he. He finally said that he was moving with me.

I had to sell my black cow that I had bought for meat but when I got her home I noticed that she had two white spots on her bag. I then knew that she was part Holstein so I had bred her with the help of the artificial insemination man. She seemed to love him. She raised her own calf and I bought another calf from the auction. She fed them both after I had taken some milk from her and she loved the two of them equally. My farm relatives in the next province laughed and laughed when they heard that I had a cow and was milking her. Since I was working shift work, the poor cow got milked one day at four p.m. and the next few days at five a.m. She didn't seem to notice. When she was in the lower pasture, I would hold up a corn stalk or a bucket and she would hurry up to the barn thinking that she was going to get something tasty to eat. Sometimes she got a tidbit, but sometimes nothing, but she always came.

This cow was full of jokes. Often she would stand sideways in her stall and that would block me in at the manger so I couldn't get out. I'm sure she was laughing. But when she raised her leg to twitch a fly, she never ever put her foot in my milk bucket. She seemed to know only how far to push me.

So I moved into my house in the city and James stayed on the farm until he sold all, every last teaspoon, of his farm contents. He came to my house with only his clothes and toiletries.

For almost thirty years, James lived in my house. He only paid for his own food and part of the utility bills. When I would ask him if he would pay me some money for living in my house and using my things, he would say that he was moving out but he never did go. He insisted on smoking in the house and put a burn on the toilet seat and a burn on my carpet. If he did any work on my house for me, I always paid him and got a receipt so that he didn't have any claim on me or my house.

James quit smoking cold turkey two times. After he stopped the first time, someone gave him a cigarette and that started him again. The second time I told him that I had purchased new white drapes and he wasn't going to smoke in the house anymore. So the smoking was finished. He had been at it a long time because his sister had taught him to smoke when he was nine years old. He had to take at least two baths a day to keep his nerves calm when he was quitting.

James worked all day fixing up the rental houses and then came home for supper. His partner didn't help very much with the work. James was good company for me even though he didn't say much.

Because I was living common law with James, my family in the next province ostracized me until I had become tired of it. So one day I said to my sister that James was rich. I said that he was not cash rich, but he was land rich. Well, they did a turn around and always said after that "How's James?" Then the mother of my son- in- law started living common law. I had been judged about it. I was amused because it is not wise to paint someone black unless you are pure yourself. My family couldn't criticize me anymore.

EIGHTEEN

On the property next door to James but above him, lived Randolph This man did wonderful cement work and when he did a basement or garage floor for you, it could not be better. Randolph was also very good at imbibing so that he wasn't much of a housekeeper. When I sold him milk and took it over to put it in his refrigerator, there was always something green growing in the refrigerator.

Randolph was growing a marijuana plant in his yard. The plant was sixteen feet high. One night the plant was stolen and gone. Two weeks later, it came back and had been replanted. The person who stole it likely did not know what to do with it so he or she brought it back.

The door to Randolph's house was always closed but unlocked. He liked us to leave our gate to his yard open so that our sheep could chew his grass and he would not have to cut it. But one day he went to work and left his door to his house open. The sheep had a hay-day. They entered the house and when Randolph came home they were sleeping on the couch and on the bed. They had made a mess all over the house.

James and I were up country for a little weekend trip. Coming home in his yellow truck it broke an axle coming down a hill. James was a good driver so his kept us from crashing. We sent a message with another driver to send a tow truck to take us farther down the hill to a garage. So we were held up two days while the truck got fixed.

We had left the daughter, Joan, at home while we were gone and she was to bottle feed a baby goat that we had bought at the auction. We had bought it because it did not have a mother and James had had goats before and liked them. So when we got home Joan said that the baby goat would not suck any milk out of the bottle that we had left. It turned out that she had picked a nipple out of the jar and had picked one that didn't have a hole in it. Of course no milk came out. The baby goat was so hungry that it went to the garden and we could see bite marks on the rhubarb leaves where the goat had eaten some bites out of the plants. The leaves of rhubarb plant contained oxalic acid which was poisonous and the baby goat died.

By this time Joan was getting married, so when James was coming to live at my house in the city there was only John to worry about. He was not home very much because he had pitched a tent in the lower part of the property and he stayed down there a lot. He could sleep until noon down there by himself and nobody bothered him.

When I was shopping for groceries one day, I was in the line to check my items out and there were two ladies ahead of me. The farthest one had a big order and was getting it through. The lady next to me whispered to me "Did you see what the checker girl did?" I replied "No, I didn't" So she told me that the checker had taken twenty dollars out of her till and put it under a piece of paper that was on the shelf covering her till. Then when the lady ahead of us was about to leave, the checker took the twenty dollars out from under the paper and put the money in her pants pocket. Then the lady who was whispering to me asked me what she should do since she had seen what was happening. I told her to tell the worker at customer service. She did and the customer service clerk's eyes got big. Inside of a minute or two, the manager was in the stall where the checker stood. He said to her "Do you want to tell me what you have done or will I roll back the camera and see for myself what you have done." The checker did not know that everything that the checkers did was on a camera tape. So she had to tell the manager. He had her empty her pants pocket and lo and behold, she had sixty dollars in twenty dollar bills in the pocket. Immediately the store security appeared, the money was recovered, and the checker was ushered out of the checking desk and out of the store. For the sake of the money, this woman had lost her job and would likely not get a good reference from the store. I thought about how she had covered for the money and concluded that she had cashed out points on three customers who were busy loading up their groceries and not watching the checker. A neat plan but she got caught.

NINETEEN

So James got settled into my house. He made his own breakfast and then went out to work all day on the rental properties. His partner seldom showed up because he was home tending to his animals on his farm. He wasn't much for getting under the rental houses to do plumbing repairs anyway or other repairs but James was good at everything. One of the renters was the fiancé of an inmate at the jail. He was in for life for murder, but like all of the prisoners he said that he didn't do it. He was let out with a guard to get married to the renter at one of James's cottages. We were invited to the wedding in the cottage. For interest, I sat beside the jail bird and asked him what it was like to be in jail and was the food good, etc. He was reluctant to tell me anything. At one point in my working life, I had applied for papers to get a job at the jail, which was a little north of my house. I had heard that the pay was good. But after I thought more about it, I decided that I did not want to work where the doors clanged and the incarcerated people all tried to con the nurse which was what I had also heard. I was still working in the Intensive Care Unit, mostly night shifts which I liked. When the nursing association had put out the first course in Intensive Care nursing, I assumed that all of the nurses had to have that course. So I thought, I might as well get with it and take the course. So I drove from Williams Lake to Kamloops to do the program for three weeks of it. Then I realized that this course was for a specialty of Intensive Care nursing and not all of the nurses had to take it. But I liked what I had learned so I stayed doing this special nursing for almost forty years. It had been worth the money and the trouble. Where I worked twenty-three years in one hospital, no one sat in the cafeteria with the ICU nurses. We sat alone to eat. One day one of the doctor's wives sat with me and noticed that I had some jam on the table. She said "Is that blackberry jam?" I replied, "Yes". So she helped herself to the jam and when she left, she took my jar of jam with her. She never even said a thank you.

When I got retired, not by my choice, and got a casual job at another hospital, I went into the cafeteria to eat and one nurse sitting at a table said to me "Here, come and sit with us". I almost dropped my lunch. I was so surprised and thought,"this is a nice place to work". I stayed working in that hospital for sixteen years. I had managed to ace the full intensive care exam that I had been given when I had first applied and that's why I got the job.

At lunch one day, one of the male nurses told us about a trip that he had taken with his male partner to the next province. He was not familiar with that province. His friend sent him to the cafe to get two coffees. When he went in, everybody had a black hat on. So he hollered out" What is this, special hat day or something?" Then he was embarrassed because he realized that the workers likely were part of a religious organization and that they always wore the black hats. He scooted out of the cafe quickly and spilled some of the coffees as he went. What was left of the coffee was good. In the hospital, at that table, we laughed so hard at what he was telling us that we could hardly eat our lunches.

After one night shift one time, I was coming out of the hospital to the parking lot when I slipped on the ice. Down onto my back I went and I managed to give the back of my head a clunk. In the funny papers that I had read as a child, the katzenjammer kids always saw stars when they got hurt. I had always thought that that was a myth. But, here I was on my back and I actually saw stars, but I didn't make it into the funny papers. My fall was not funny at all.

After James got settled into my house, we were both out driving separately one day and both of us, unbeknown to the other one, saw a used camper that would go onto James's truck. Funny enough we both found the same camper. When we talked about that camper, we decided to buy it for $1500 dollars, $ 750 dollars each. When we had it home, I did a few repairs to it to make it good. I climbed onto the roof and put sealer onto the roof seams, fixed the stove burners, put new screening over the windows where the screen had been pushed out, and oiled the door. I made up the bed and put rugs on the floor. I also added some 5 gallon jugs to carry water so we wouldn't have to carry a tank full of water. I also put in a small electric heater so we could run it when we were paying for power. Then we added a few things like special plugs and cooking things as we went along.

I also put in my axe and some blocks if we needed them to level the camper, and a small green stool so I could get up and through the door easily. I had purchased this stool at a garage sale in my city where the parents had been killed on the highway coming home from the theater of the sister city across the bridge. These parents died instantly when hit by a driver running a red light at the intersection and they left at home many children. The house contents were now being sold and the children were taken to live with their aunt and uncle.

When the camper got settled into my carport after it had been lowered down by the turn handles that let it down onto the saw horses, we decided that we could go someplace about every two months but after the first of the month when James collected the rents.

One of the first trips that we made was to visit a nurse classmate of mine. She lived in Los Gatos, California. I had phoned her to ask her if we could come to visit. She was thrilled that a Canadian friend was coming to visit. She was Canadian but her husband, a teacher, was American. We took my son with us. I was driving because the traffic was heavy as we neared San Francisco and I was complaining about the many lanes of traffic. James said, "Wait until we get south of San Francisco and there will be fewer lanes of traffic". What a joke. There were still ten lanes going south.

When we were at her house her husband complained a lot about his wife, my friend, working all of her life at nursing, but did not have a pension from it. What did they expect? She had done private duty nursing as an independent all of the time to get the higher wage, but no pension. You can't have it two ways. This man had a large case that stood on end and opened up to display his large coin collection. He said he was the largest coin dealer in the United States and he took the case and showed the coins at many shows. His wife had never had and was not interested in dolls as a child, but now she had a large doll collection and teddy bears. She also did shows as a hobby. She was very kind and gave my boy who was twelve at the time, a medium sized teddy bear. My boy is now a man in his forties and I don't know if he still has the bear or not.

My friend was used to the heavy traffic of San Francisco so she offered to take us north into the city. We saw the cable cars travelling up and down Market Street. They always had a strong man in the cars to work the brake leaver so the car would not go too fast or run away. If you wanted to ride the tram, you had to jump on quickly because the cable car did not really come to a complete stop. The cars went all the way up to Nob Hill where the better houses were and at the bottom they were turned around at Fisherman's Wharf by being on a large cement turn table. They then went back up Market Street. The cable cars were a big attraction for tourists as was Fisherman's Wharf where there were stalls that sold fresh fish and lobster newly out of the sea. From that area you could look out to see the Golden Gate Bridge, the Bay Bridge, the prison Alcatraz, and the large expanse of San Francisco Bay. My son was thrilled with it all. We had come over the Golden Gate Bridge to get into the city.

Once, a long time before, I had been on a vacation with my mother to see San Francisco and when we were there, I persuaded my mother to let us go to the matinee of the live performance of Louis Armstrong. I was at the age where the music made a big impression on me and I have since thought how lucky I was to hear him play from a big stage. This was the thrill of a lifetime for me.

TWENTY

In my neighbourhood where James and I lived, the neighbours did interesting things. Across the street, a couple decided that their two boys, ages twelve and thirteen, were watching too much T.V. So they gave the T.V. to charity. No more T.V., they thought. But the smart boys then went from school to houses of their friends to watch the screens. My neighbours were upset. So they had to buy another T.V. Next thing that I could see in my peeping Tom role, was the family sitting on the couch in front of a T.V. screen and they had plates of food in their laps. It was from the ridiculous to the sublime. This was the only way that they could solve the situation and keep the boys home.

A neighbour a little farther down the street wanted me to paint her portrait. I said that I would have to take some pictures of her, which I did. When the portrait was finished, I showed it to some of my artist friends and they said it was perfect. So I phoned her and told her that I would bring it over and that I would only like ninety dollars for it. This price was a steal. When I got to her house, she had a friend with her. The two of them must have discussed the price and I assume that she did not want to pay at all, thinking that it was going to be free because I had said that I liked painting portraits. I also assumed that the friend had told her that if she didn't want to pay for it, to tell me that she didn't like it. I was walking into a trap. When she saw the portrait she said what only came out of her mouth four different times, was that she didn't like it. This lady had raised four grown up boys and surely one of them would have liked to have a portrait of their mother. If she had not said four times that she didn't like it, I would even have given it to her free, but no way now. So I took the portrait home, kept it for six months in case she changed her mind, then cut it up with great glee and put a new canvas on the stretcher bars. I made up my mind that after that, any other portrait was going to be paid before I painted it.

One neighbour a few blocks away had a husband who did woodworking in his carport. He had a shed on the front property line, not five feet into his yard like the bylaw asked for. It contained a lot of electric and other tools. It was locked. This couple didn't have any children or a dog, big or small. One night the husband heard a noise outside near his locked shed. He went out and accosted a youth trying to get into his shed to steal tools. They had quite an argument. Then the boy said that he was going home to get his brother and that they would be back. A short time later, there again was a noise at the front of his house where the shed was. Out he went. The two youths this time were again trying to jimmy the lock to get the tools in the shed. There wasn't an argument this time because the brother had a shotgun with him and shot the owner. Bang and the owner was dead. Then they took what they wanted. Now, because of this incident, they were wanted by the police.

After the funeral, the wife's brother came to live with his sister in the house. He took what was left of the tools into the house and demolished the shed. He also removed the small fence at the front of the property. The lady also got a fairly big dog, a poodle that seemed very friendly. Who would think that two youths would shoot a resident in a city just to get some tools.

Next to that house lived a couple with two almost grown children. The son was not home one evening but the husband, wife, and daughter were home. Around supper time the wife, daughter, and dog got into her car and left in a hurry and only had their purses with them. The next day, I talked to the lady who was a friend of mine and asked her what had happened. She said that she had left her husband a couple of times before, but each time had gone back. This time she was not going back. She told me that her husband who always seemed nice to me had come on heavily with her and her daughter. So they had had to get away quickly without any of their belongings. The husband refused to give them any of their things but when they each got a lawyer the husband was told to give his daughter her things but not the wife's things.

The wife and daughter had found a small apartment to rent and it had a ground level patio door so it was perfect for the dog to go in and out. The other tenants liked the dog so there was not a problem. My basement tenant had moved out by then, and I had decided that I was not renting to anyone anymore as that tenant and a few others had caused me problems. In that room was a full kitchen. I picked out some things that my friend and her daughter could use for their place. Then I went twice to a U.S. big box store and bought everything that she would need to outfit the kitchen. She still had a good job so was able to get some clothes and other necessities. Much later she and the daughter went to live with a male friend that she had known in grade school. I miss her and the dog next door to me because she was always happy to get any extra vegetables that I had to spare from my garden. I was never going to give the husband any vegetables. My friend did not say exactly why they had left their home so fast but I thought that maybe the husband had had a weapon, and had threatened to kill them. No one ever knows what goes on behind closed doors.

A neighbour kiddy- corner south of my house used to come over every year, uninvited, and pick the pears that were low down on the side of my pear tree that was facing her house. One day I was in her yard talking with her and I spied a large growth of mint in her garden. So I told her that I did not have any mint. After all of the pears that she had had, she did not offer me any part of her mint plant.

So the next spring, I went to her house and said "Please don't pick any more of my pears because I have people who come, pick them, and take them to the women's shelter". The game was now even. I didn't get any mint but she didn't get any more pears.

One other neighbour came to my door and told me that he now had a tractor with a blade on it and he would clear the snow from my drive for free. I thanked him but told him that I would keep paying the neighbour children a small amount to do the driveway because I felt that they had to learn to work, but I thanked him anyway.

We only get snow in our area four or five times a year and sometimes it melts as soon as it falls. One year when we had a heavy snowfall, and the town's grader put a lot of snow from other driveways onto the front of my drive. I had cleared my driveway so there was a big space to accept his blade's snow. The pile that he made was over three feet high and packed. There wasn't any hope of me getting my car out until spring when it would melt. I should have called the town office and made the driver come back and clear it but I never thought of doing that. So I shovelled and shovelled for almost three hours to get the pile low enough so I could drive over the amount that was left. I had taken a photo of the big pile dumped in front of my car. The photo showed my car and the huge pile. Then I sent the picture and a letter to the town so that that would never happen again and it didn't.

TWENTY ONE

When James came home every night for supper after doing a day's work, he would come into the house and holler, "What's on at the show?" Sometimes I would say that we had seen all the shows but he had other alternatives. He liked not only the theater in the city across the bridge, but he liked to eat downtown in our town or to go travelling especially with the camper. The theatre in our town had closed out. The senior owner had died and left the cinema to his daughter who was also a projectionist. After a while she was tired of running it alone so she sold it to a book man who brought hundreds of used books to our town. I tried to buy some books from him, but the place was not very tidy and he was a long time coming from the back of the store to the front to wait on me. He wasn't very interested in selling books. I left without buying anything and never went back. One of my friends asked this owner if he had a book on customer relations. He said that he did have a book like that so she told him that he should read it.

So the fact that James liked to do things is what I liked about him and that was what I missed the most after he died. He always wanted to go to every show, eat out, or travel. He had never been out of the province until he had met me, and he enjoyed seeing new places.

I had air miles to spend and I told him that we would fly as far as we could in Canada to get the most out of the air miles. He was happy to help me use up my perks.

The farthest that we could go was to Newfoundland. The first time that we went there was for three days and we liked the province. The people were very friendly. Then we went a second time and stayed a week to see the whole province. When we were at the counter to rent the car that I had booked, the counter lady had a trainee beside her. When we were about to leave, I said," Where is my credit card?" I looked right at the trainee and she reached into her drawer in front of herself and took out my credit card. She was stealing it. We were lucky to have a rental car because all of the motels were booked and the first night in that province I drove until ten p.m. looking for a place to stay. We finally got a motel away out in the country.

On the next morning I said that we were going to buy some sleeping bags and sleep in the car because I couldn't drive so late and drive all day too. Newfoundland, we thought, was a safe and honest place to be, except for the trainee at the rental car booth at the airport.

When at a hardware store, we found sleeping bags that we liked. I asked the owner how much they would be if we bought two. His eyes got big because he couldn't believe his luck that we would buy more than one. With those bags, we did sleep in the car and I said at least we were lucky enough to have a rental car as the radio said that there weren't any more rental cars available.

We continued on to see all of the peninsulas of that province. When we were in the hamlet of Fortune, all eyes got wide when people looked at me. I was a Bonnell and my forefathers had been from Newfoundland from Fortune and Lamaline but there were also other Bonnells throughout the province. I looked like a Bonnell for sure and I looked very much like some of the local people that we met. In Fortune, I visited a lady who was researching all of the families of the province, including the Bonnells. She told me a lot about my ancestors which helped me with my genealogy papers that I had been working on for several years. She also sent me to visit, in Fortune, a cousin of mine that I hadn't known about. We had a nice time together for a few hours.

When we were flying home, the man in the seat next to us said that he had paid sixteen hundred dollars for his plane seat. We didn't tell him that both of us were flying free with air miles.

After that trip, we started going to Mexico. I only booked the trips for one week's stay because I wanted to know that we were going to get home in a week if one of us got sick. Two weeks was too long. Luckily we only got the runs once and got them cleared up quickly when we got home. On one trip when we were unpacking at home, a large spider crawled out of a vase that we had purchased. He didn't last long in my house.

We went to Mexico eight times, each time to a different place except we went twice to Mazatland and twice to Guadalajara, a university city. We saw many interesting things in Mexico. I had learned moderate Spanish at the college and with the help of some work books, so we could get around well. James stuck to me like glue because I could speak fairly well and he could only say thanks and beer in Spanish.

One day we were walking and after quite a while I noticed that we were walking out of the town. We were quite far away. So we hurried back because it was not safe to be away from the town by ourselves. In the town, we also saw things that we thought were interesting.

There was an old truck parked on a street. It looked like it had been there for a long time. When the town workers came along and were painting the curb white, they painted right across the old trucks tires. We also thought that it was unusual that fence slats and fence posts outlining some of the lots were made out of sturdy cactus trunks but that worked.

When we were in one town, we had attended a program in the town square in the afternoon. When the outing was over, all of the Mexican people moved to the side of the square, except for us. We remained standing in the centre of the plaza. Pretty soon, the people at the side started waving at us. We waved back. This waving went on for several minutes then someone came over to us and spoke in English to tell us that the army was waiting at the sidelines to come into the square and do some drills that they did every day at five p.m. We didn't know that and were in the way. How embarrassing for us, but we moved.

One evening we were sitting in a cafe eating supper. A Mexican lady, middle aged, came over to us and tried to sell James a rose for me. He declined to buy it by nodding his head. So I said to the woman in Spanish "Me esposo es un codo". Both she and I laughed. What I had said was "My husband is a codo". A codo in Mexico is a person from northern Mexico who is very cheap. James never found out what I had said. He should have gone to Spanish classes with me.

On another trip to Mexico, we stayed at a gated community with lots of houses. We had rented one. It was furnished but had bugs around the kitchen counter. We spoke to the manager of the complex and he said that the bugs came with the territory and we would not get rid of them. We were not pleased. James was sitting on the couch one afternoon and he had his feet on the coffee table. He accidentally bumped a wooden flower ornament on that table. The ornament flew apart into many pieces. He had broken it. What were we going to do? So I picked up the pieces and realized that the flower in the pot could be put back together by tucking the pieces into place and I got it fixed. We didn't like staying in that house because it was a long walk to get out to the bus that we had to catch to get to town to get some meals. We weren't going to cook where there were bugs as we were not used to that.

On another trip, we got a local bus at the Mexican City airport and went south to Pueblo. That town was old and had had an earthquake several years prior. What was surprising was that the buildings damaged by the earthquake were not yet restored. When would they get to them? While there, I tried to look up a previous Spanish teacher that I had had in Canada, but couldn't locate either her or her father who was a doctor. They lived in Pueblo and it was strange, I thought, that I could not even locate her doctor father.

We always got along well in Mexico because I could speak a fair amount of Spanish. When we went to buy something, we always got a better price, I thought, because I could bargain. I also helped out a lot of tourists who needed assistance. Once on a bus, I helped a young man get his change back from the attendant who travelled with the driver. So I said to the young man" You owe me big time". When the bus came to the end of the line and we all got off, the young man and his partner scooted away from the bus as fast as they could go. I think he was afraid that I was going to ask him for something. That's the last thing that crossed my mind. What I had said was only a well used saying.

After James got sick, we couldn't go to Mexico any more. I missed those trips because each time that I landed in Mexico and all the signs were in Spanish, my language skills kicked right in and I felt at home. Also, I tried to speak only Spanish while there in order to practice. I was also advised that it was now not safe to go to Mexico. That is why we never toured Mexico City because it was known to be unsafe even in the tourist taxis. I imagine that if you lived in Mexico City the bad people didn't bother you, but they can spot the tourists a mile or more away.

TWENTY TWO

After the camper trip to California, we didn't take my son on any more trips in the camper because he had to go to school. But James and I went all over Canada and the United States. My sister heard, likely from me, that we were going to go to Phoenix. Well, she was bound and determined that since she had not been there before, she was coming with us to Phoenix. So I would have to pick her up in the next province and deliver her back there at the end of the trip. My son- in- law told me to put a stop to that notion right away because she talked non-stop and would drive us crazy. So I talked with her and told her that it was James and my time together and she wouldn't like the way that we travelled. I also told her that we were skirting Phoenix to avoid the big city. When I told her that while travelling, at lunch time, we often pulled in and I put a paper towel on the table for a plate so we could make a sandwich. Well, I got a lecture on how we were hurting the environment by using paper towels that way. How many paper towels did she use in her home?

I always thought that my sister was the strange one in the family and so did other people. My cousin said to me one day," How are you two sisters and are so different?"

Thank goodness that I was not like her, I thought. When her two small grandchildren came to her house to visit, she only let them play on a small rug at the front door or on the three foot square landing halfway down to her basement. If a toy fell off the rug, they got scolded because her hardwood floors had been sanded so much that they couldn't be done again. I got thinking about that situation so I told her son to put a stop to it because she was abusing his children. I never fathomed how she could treat little ones the way she did especially her own grandchildren.

When we were visiting in the city where my sister lived, she took us to her church. In the middle of the service one time, there was a lady singing a solo at the front and I was sitting next to an old man. I noticed that the old man didn't seem to be breathing. So I felt his pulse and there wasn't one. So, being an Intensive Care Nurse, I shook him and said in a very loud voice, in case he was deaf, "Take a deep breath". The soloist stopped singing and took a big breath as did the entire congregation. When the old man came conscious, I managed to help him to the back of the church to a couch that was there. His wife came also, and she gave him some nitro and he revived. I decided after that that I wasn't going to go to that church again because there were too many old people that went there.

When we were in the United States, I noticed that the people did not do any recycling even for pop cans. So when I got home, I wrote a letter to their president to tell him that we could not find anyone who would take our pop cans to recycle them. Within the next year, the U.S. started doing some recycling. So someone read my letter.

We took the camper and went two times across Canada. When we had to get gas in Quebec, we filled up and when I went to pay I realized that the lady manning the till only spoke French. I assumed that she might be hostile to English speaking people so I said to her in Spanish "Soy Espanol". She didn't understand so I said it again"I am Spanish". Then a big smile came over her face as she had understood. When we were pulling out of the gas station, she was still standing at the door and watching us. There was still a big beaming smile across her whole face. I had made her day!

We enjoyed seeing the Maritime Provinces as the people there were friendly and relaxed. We were shown in one of the provinces, a small church that had been built in one day by some Irish workmen. The men worked hard and fast to get the church finished by nightfall because they thought that they were building a pub.

When in the United States on our trips, we went twice to Mississippi where my son and his wife were at university. I wanted to get some photos of local people sitting on their porches but my son said that I was not to go over the railway tracks because it would not be safe for me to do so. The next best thing that I could do was to take pictures of James sitting on my son's porch pretending to knit. It would be easy to put a dress on him and make him into what I wanted for a painting.

When the other coaches saw a new red Mustang parked in my son's driveway, they all came to the door to ask if my son had come into a windfall. He told them it was his mother's rental car. I had to be careful while driving that car because it went like the blazes with me only putting a light foot on the gas pedal. The police couldn't miss a red car especially if it was speeding.

When we were on another trip with the camper, James wanted to see Montana, so we went there. When we got to Montana, I said "Well, here it is". There was nothing to see except rolling hills. We did manage to go to most of the cities to see them. In the bare landscape there would only be cowboys and herds but we didn't see many of them.

James also wanted to see Texas, so we went there twice and stayed in El Paso. We were near the Rio Grande River and the border to Mexico. In the daytime we took the Border Jumper trolley into Mexico and it took us around in Juarez. The trolley was for tourists. Every place that the trolley stopped, the Mexicans would try to sell us something but since we were only there for the day, we did not bite. When we were in the camper every night and were camped near the river, we heard volleys of shots. They continued on until almost dawn. We never saw any trouble in the daytime, but this was the evening's past time.

I never thought that I would get to see Graceland or New Orleans, but when my son and wife were working in Mississippi, my son took us to these places. We couldn't go into the graveyard in New Orleans because hobos lived there and would attack us because we were in their territory. However, down by the levee we sent my son over to the booth for the stern wheeler tours on the Mississippi River to inquire as to the price. Since it was reasonable we went on the boat and the price included music and lunch. The river here was at a different level than the city which was protected by dykes. On Beale Street in New Orleans we got to see the music shops and hear some blues music by street musicians.

When in Graceland we were taken on a tour of Elvis's house and saw all his famous memorabilia. The graves were there of him and his parents but to this day I am not sure that Elvis was in one because there have been too many sightings of him elsewhere. In the U.S., there is a small museum that a man runs that is called "Elvis is Alive". He makes a living with that theme and has lots of indications that Elvis didn't die when the press said he did. I recall that there weren't any pictures of him dead or in a coffin. At that time, his father was his manager and I'm sure that he wasn't going to let his son die. There were other ways of which I can think of how the situation could have been handled. With a new identity and his vocal cords cut, Elvis could never sing again. The singing would be how he would be found. If he was still alive, he must have been amused at all the Elvis impersonators around, some of whom are very skilled.

Coming home from the south, we stopped late one night at a camp site a little north of Oklahoma City. I went to the closed office and there was not a drop box to leave money so we backed the camper up to a fence that was a proper spot and went to sleep. At two a. m. there was pounding on our little door and it frightened us half to death. The manager of the camp site was making the noise and he wanted money because he said that other people camped there and took off early in the morning and skipped out with not paying. We said that we had looked for a drop box but didn't find one and that we certainly were going to pay in the morning. In the early morning the owner was standing at his door with his hand out waiting for the money. I made a mental note to never again stay near Oklahoma City.

TWENTY THREE

When we were driving, we always had to make sure that I was driving before each city so that I could do the driving in the traffic. James was traffic shy, but was fine on the highway. We didn't understand why lots of people went by us, honked and waved. We had bought the camper as used and it had some stickers on the back. One of the stickers read "Easy Does It". Then it dawned on us that that was a slogan we thought was used by the alcoholics association. When people waved at us, we always waved back so that the other people would feel acknowledged.

We had gone across Canada twice to see the whole country. The drive around the north side of Lake Superior was very long with just the lake to see.

Then a few months later, James wanted to go again across Canada. I told him that I did not want to go as it took too long and I had other things to do. I also told him that he was not taking my half of the camper. I heard nothing more, until one day I got a message on the answering machine that was from a trailer shop across the bridge and west on the highway. The message said that they had received on their lot a camper that would fit James's truck but that he would need to buy three belly straps to go under the truck to hold the camper down. They would rent the camper to him.

I knew that James was having coffee every day and oftener with one of his tenants who was the age of his daughter. This woman, when younger, used to come to his farm to see his daughter so I knew her and knew her age. So now she would often phone to my house to speak with James, but he was always out. I was like a receptionist for him because I answered the phone and took the messages. That was free service for James and I never ever got a "thanks" for it.

On our last trip to Mexico, James had bought six colorful shirts. They hung in our closet but almost every week one of them would be in the wash basket but I never ever saw him wear that shirt. Suddenly the light struck me that he was wearing the shirts to visit this young tenant. That, with the fact of the message about the rented camper to go on his truck, brought me to the conclusion that he was going to go across Canada without me but with this young lady. Since there was only one bed in the camper plus the seat behind the table for a bed, they would no doubt be sleeping in the comfortable bed over the cab. I was not happy and was not going to let all of this happen.

So I took the six new shirts to the Thrift Store across the river and donated them all. I did not give them away in our town in case James saw them on someone else. James must have realized that the shirts were gone but didn't say a word. He knew why they were gone.

So to put a stop to him going to go away with this young thing, I said that I would take some holidays and would go with him.

Part way along the road with James driving, I said to him"Well, is your affair over?"His only reply was that it was "the thrill of the chase".

James also wanted to try out every new thing that he hadn't done before. So when some ladies of the street came into our city, James had to test them out. He was dumb enough to come home and tell me about it, I guess to relieve his conscience. Did he think that I would say "Well done" or something to that effect. What I said to him was that that was a good way to get a disease. I chalked his misbehaviour up to a mid life crisis or whatever it is that men get.

At one time James talked with his partner and said that he wanted to leave me. His partner told him that he was crazy to think that way. So he stayed at my house not paying anything to live with me and at the same time have the use of all of my things.

One of the renters that James and his partner had had was a lady who had been a big executive in the East, so she had made lots of money in her life. Recently, she had been married to a farmer in the West but she had left him. When she left, she took everything that was not nailed down including a toilet, a basin, and all kinds of tools that she would never use, much less know what to do with them.

All that she took plus all the things that she had bought for herself, like shoes still in boxes, and clothes were stacked to the ceiling in the little house that she was renting from James and his partner. There was only a walking path through the house. The lady had gone to live at her daughter's house in another town and the daughter said that the articles could be disposed of. So the men had two garage sales but that did not deal with half of the stored stuff.

I felt sorry for James so I went to the cottage to help him and his partner. Some of the walls had to be washed to the ceiling with bleach because of the articles stacked so high without air so there was mold. The partner took to washing those walls. I bleached the bathroom all over to get rid of the mold. Then I worked on the kitchen. I was cleaning the double sink when my hand went through the metal at the bottom of the sink. So that finished the sink. With a lot of further work, the house was able to be put back to normal and was ready for renting again.

As James got older, he started to get sick with bad circulation especially in his legs. He had smoked for about fifty years. So one night he told me to sell the camper but I said that I liked it and didn't want to sell it. Then the next year he told me again to sell the camper. This time I did.

Only two men, partners, came to see it and they bought it. I had set the price at five hundred dollars which was a bargain. I sold it complete but should have taken some of the things out of it because when the men loaded the camper up and left, I found that they had stolen the pile of cut wood that was in my carport. I was keeping the wood in case the power went out for a long time.

We had paid fifteen hundred dollars for the camper and I had put the selling price at five hundred dollars. That camper had served us handsomely for almost thirty years for the thousand dollars that it had cost us after we got five hundred dollars as the selling price. The camper had outlived four trucks and had taken us all over the country.

After the camper was gone, someone said to me "Why do you park in front of the carport instead of in it?" Then I realized that the habit of parking in front of the carport when the camper was always in it was still strong in my mind.

It wasn't long after that that James died and my travelling days were over.

TWENTY FOUR

Over the years, I had made several trips back to the outpost hamlet to visit my family and I saw the area change from the outpost to a town and then to a city. After many years of research, the oil companies were working the oil sands and the place was booming. On the way there, I stopped in a town where my roommate from nursing school lived and stayed there for a few days then went cross country to the northern highway. My son had told me not to travel that highway on a weekend as it would be bumper to bumper traffic both in and out of the city. The road had been built over the muskeg and it stood up to the heavy traffic.

When in the town, my son would drive me around to show me all the newer subdivisions that had sprung up since my last visit. His wife sold real estate for about a year, but stopped doing it because houses were so much in demand that she would get called out in the middle of the night so the people could make their deal right then. She couldn't handle the night calls.

I saw the hamlet get more and more amenities like a newer and bigger school, a new hospital and more and more businesses. A man that I knew had a commercial lot in the now city and opened a bar and grill. Men who worked at the oil sands often rented a room in a resident's home and paid big bucks to do so. But, they had to get their supper elsewhere. So they liked to eat at the bar and grill. Sometimes the hungry people would be lined up out the door to wait for their supper. That business was not the only one that was prospering in the boom.

The city was also getting newer stores and fast food outlets. The big box stores were coming to roost there and they were popular. So the shopping and dining was improving almost daily. If it had been like that when I lived there, I might not have left. I never regretted leaving because I made a much more interesting life for myself away from the outpost and I was able to use my education in my field. I had to support myself, but I usually liked my work.

So the northern outpost was fast fading. The people who had lived there in that time were gone to other places or gone to the big outpost in the sky. We remembered some of them from their names on the street signs. Many of them who had property, sold their holdings for quite a lot of money.

About three hundred head of buffalo still roam on the large amount of land north of the city but that land where they are, is now fenced. The people of the next northern town don't have to get their mail and goods by barge, plane or by truck over a winter road. The teachers who go there now do not have to order their year's supply of food at one time.

Since there now is a road built from the mainland of the city to McDonald's Island, the snye instead of being a waterway with flowing water is damned up and has become more like a slough. The float planes and the local boats still use it but it is not the same. Perhaps big culverts could have been put in under the road so water could keep the snye water moving. I guess no one thought of that. I should have been an engineer.

Across the bridge going to the north and to one of the big oil companies, the hill is called Supertest Hill. Buses take a lot of workers from the city, over that road in and out every day so they can work at the oil sands.

The city now has mail delivered into boxes on the corners and there is garbage pickup. Animals like rabbits and deer still come wandering into the city especially through the area up on the hill to the west. We used to travel the roads up there to have a drive and to shoot rabbits. Now there are subdivisions where we used to go. It would not be prudent to try to shoot rabbits in the subdivisions.

The fresh food is available every day instead of coming on the train once a week. The weekly water truck is replaced by pipes for the city's water supply.

The roads going out of town are now all season roads and the road going south has been mastered over the muskeg. Some people don't know what muskeg is but in the past the soggy ground limited the travel to the train. But in the winter when the area was frozen there was a road built over the muskeg. However, that road had its disadvantages. One was that there was a deep dip down where the road went and a climb to get up out of the low spot. Usually residents went two cars together to help each other climb that hill. I never liked going over that road especially if I had my children with me. It was usually touch and go to get up that steep hill in the snow. People of the outpost always helped each other especially if it meant keeping them from freezing on a lone road.

The house that had the tea wagon with the silver tea set on top of it has been moved to an outdoor museum. The caboose of the train is also at the museum as are some of the stores with well known store fronts. These artifacts are reminders of the outpost that the city used to be, but if you had not lived there the effect would not be the same.

The new hospital is not an F class hospital anymore. I wonder if it has an enema tray and a stretcher to take the labor patients to the delivery room. There is more than one doctor so the nurse does not have to cover for the only doctor when that doctor used to go out on the weekends to the bigger city. There is also more than one bank, more than one gas station, and more churches than just the Roman Catholic Church and the Anglican Church. There are still baby showers and wedding showers but since the city is so big, the attendants are by invitation only as not everybody knows all of the people in the entire city.

The winters remain severe but if you are making good money, you try not to notice. A lot of the people there are used to the climate and mostly they are hardy folk.

Much has happened over the years. Now the province is smiling because the hopes and dreams of the northern outpost have come into reality.

The research has paid off and the oil companies can now produce a steady stream of oil. The developers must feel very proud.

The winters are still as cold as ever, sometimes even getting to minus 55 degrees below zero, but the living in the area is easier since there is prosperity. The abundance of new stores helps a lot.

In the olden times, I always bundled up my children in the winter and took them outside every day. I thought that the outdoor weather made them hardy. What used to be in the time of the Northern Outpost is like a dream and is only remembered by the people who were there. That dream has now evolved into a modern city and the Northern Outpost is gone forever but the memories remain.

Manufactured by Amazon.ca
Bolton, ON

34285878R00087